EVP and New Dimensions

Alexander MacRae

Sanctuary Press

Third Edition 2004

Sanctuary Press

Table of Contents

What else is common to EVP?

3) "Spookiness"

Most people when they hear EVP for the first time are inclined to say things like 'It made the hair at the back of my neck stand on end' or 'It gave me the cold shivers'; somehow one senses that there is something kind of spooky about it.

Fortunately, or unfortunately, those spooky feelings dont last – it soon becomes quite normal.

That is how it is in the early stages – it feels – "spooky." But you can't really make a definition out of that. It doesn't happen for everyone, and it wears off after a while. So this is not really a scientific definition – to do that you would need to back it up with experiments, but we are working on it.

And there you have the basic definitions of EVP and the main things that characterize it.

EVP is about hearing voices. But I am not going to get into what the voices say – not just yet. I have seen so many people being led astray by that – and leading others astray in their turn. Don't believe everything you hear.

There are some that tend to define EVP by what they believe they hear the voices saying – and often what they hear is what they expect to hear.

If they hear a voice saying, 'This is the Great God Metallicus talking to you' – they believe that EVP is the Great God Metallicus's private radio network, and according to them, there are whole teams of Metallicians up there in Astral City broadcasting to us.

That is what they want you to believe, but, somehow, I dont think so.

Hearing Voices

Lets look at the question of hearing voices. This is an important question for anyone doing EVP. For the uninformed there could be risks in getting involved in doing this. That some do – and don't come to any harm, is a point, but I think that most people would agree that EVP does have its fair share of people who could be classified as schizophrenic. Go out on the Web and listen to some of the samples. Some are very *imaginative.*

How do we know that the voices are not just conjurations of our mind – illusions we get attached to – illusions which we believe to be real, on which our survival and status depend – so much so that we become quite frantic if anyone questions them.

How do we know that they are real? Well, first we have to be courageous enough to look at the possibility that they may not be spirit-voices – they might just be "auditory hallucinations"

We will spend time on this question, it won't be easy but it will be worth it. Spirit voices or auditory hallucinations?

Voices as sources of conflict

Dont think we are the first to have heard voices of unknown origin. Hearing voices – without any equipment – goes back a long way.

Lets look at the Dark Side for a moment.

Hitler, according to his own account, communed with what he called Dark Forces, with the ancient god, Wotan, which he believe empowered him.

And look what damage that caused.

The French teenager, Joan of Arc, listened to what she believed were the voices of Saints and following their instructions started the Great War of her time, the Hundred Years war – in the belief that she was right.

According to one source – and you are not supposed to know this, there are people in high places today that believe that they have a pretty direct line to God – and can't wait for Armageddon to start – to prove that they were right. The only way they can be right is to kill everybody who is wrong.

Operators and Things

In the late fifties a strange new book was published. It was republished in 1976 but is now out of print although copies can be found. Unfortunately I no longer have my copy and so for what follows I am greatly indebted to Bobby Matherne for permission to use extensive quotes from his on-line review of "Operators and Things." [1]

The reason I am going to write a few paragraphs about this book is to serve as a caution that though EVP can and should be enjoyable – it should not be treated irresponsibly. You saw above how some voices can lead to conflict. Now we are going to consider another conflict – the conflict within.

EVP lies at a crossover point in human Evolution. It is a much more important activity than it might seem to those who regard it as merely "paranormal" or "bizarre."

A wise man once said that what was in God's mind when he made this universe was Evolution, and – look around – what is going on?

Evolution.

I will now refer to Bobby Matherne's review.

> "Operators and Things" is basically a story in the life of a young lady called Barbra O'Brien.

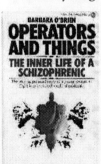

The subtitle of the book was "The Inner Life of a Schizophrenic."

And that best describes the theme of the book.

"'Operators" is O'Brien's name for beings that live inside her head as part of her unconscious processes, processes which for her are made conscious during her schizophrenia.

O'Brien's Book

---

[1] You can read the original at
http://www.doyletics.com/_arj1/operator.htm.

The name "Operator" is given by an "Operator" to itself – to distinguish itself from a "Thing."

A "Thing" is the normally conscious part of a person that is manipulated, out of its awareness, by an operator.

Thus "operators and things" refer to the complete set of unconscious and conscious processes laid bare for us by a "crazy" person who became privy to the workings of both aspects of her mind during a trip into insanity and back into sanity.'

Apparently what is going on is a sort of game played by the operators where they try to score points by causing a person to become emotional or two people to become emotional and, if possible – golden points – to get in conflict with each other.

The trip to sanity was on a Greyhound bus – a mode of transportation chosen by her operator Hinton as the safest method of living in the sane world as a schizophrenic. One can travel on a bus, ignoring fellow passengers, being in a daze, acting slightly odd and be completely unbothered by fellow passengers.

'Her trip takes her to San Francisco after a stop at a mountain cabin and a close encounter with Indians and a mountain lion. She retreats to an apartment building in which her solitude is invaded by beings who invade her mind from neighboring apartments – Grandma who gives her medical advice and the Western Boys who "scallop her latticework" and leave her "dummetized."

A glossary of terms is dictated to her by an "Operator" and is included in the appendix for the reader.

Out of the fantasy she emerges – six months later, sane. In addition she adds to the store of literature on schizophrenia a rare, first-person account of a trip so many people take but so few return from.'

I have included quite a lot about this book as a caution against the quick, glib assumption that everything that happens in

EVP is explicable within spiritualist philosophy as it is
currently known.

Talking to the Voices

And here is someone else who has something to say on the
subject. His name is Dr. Wilson Van Dusen. When he wrote
his book 'The Presence of Spirits in Madness' he was Chief
Psychologist at Mendocino State Hospital in California where
he worked among the mentally ill for 17 years.

In his book he wrote,

> 'By an extraordinary series of circumstances a
> confirmation appears to have been found for one of
> Emanuel Swedenborg's[2] more unusual doctrines that
> man's life depends on his relationship to a hierarchy of
> spirits.'

He then describes how he got the patients who were aware of
their hallucinations to describe to him their hallucinations and
in fact to get in contact through the patient with the sources of
the voices. He continues,

> 'One consistent finding was that patients felt they had
> contact with another world or order of beings.'

It would be advisable for anyone taking up EVP research on a
professional or group basis to ensure that at least one of those
involved had read Dr. Van Dusen's book. This is a real
scientist, with real experience, and he has things to say that are
very relevant to our work. We don't have to agree with him
but it would be most unwise to ignore what he has to say.

There are some that should not get involved in EVP – unless
through a qualified practitioner, and these are,

- those who already hear voices,

- those who feel they have to prove to the world that they
  are right,

---

[2] Emmanuel Swedenborg was a famous Swedish Scientist who late in his life
undertook spiritual research – investigating the Beyond centuries before our
time.

- those who have emotional, nervous or mental situations to handle.

Just to reassure anyone who hears voices – hearing voices does not in itself mean that a person has a psychological problem. There is an association of people who hear voices who are not in any way psychologically disturbed. You can check it out on the Net.

And – no – I have never heard any voices, personally.

However, the condition known as schizophrenia affects a growing number of young people. For men the peak age group is 18 years to 25 for the onset of schizophrenia. For women the peak age group extends from 25 to 30, with a very small sub-group up at 40.

In schizophrenia the person who has the condition is apt to hear voices. This condition is best discussed with the professionals in that field.

And here, this time from Spain, is a clinical study which shows some of the similarities the condition has to EVP. The following are quotes from "BEHAVIOURAL TREATMENT OF AUDITORY HALLUCINATIONS IN A SCHIZOPHRENIC PATIENT: A CASE STUDY" by Drs Salvador Perona-Garcelan and Carlos Cuevas-Yust, of the Rehabilitation Unit of "Virgen del Rocio" (Sevilla). The quotes are taken from, VOLUME 2. NUMBER 1. 1998. PSYCHOLOGY IN SPAIN.

'Functional analysis of the auditory hallucinations

The auditory hallucinations, according to the patient, consisted in hearing the voices of people who were not present at that moment, or who had died. They were short sentences or words with a content formed generally of insults or comments showing annoyance directed towards him, for example "get lost", "you're mad", "you're an idiot", "drop dead", etc. He attributed the voices to a friend who was killed in a car accident several years before, or to a neighbor from the flat above. He said that both the dead friend and the neighbor wanted to make his life unbearable, and that the latter was aware of his every move.'

OK - out of that, note the following,

- Hearing the voices of people ... who had died.
- Short sentences or words.
- Generally of insults or comments showing annoyance directed towards him.

Sounds pretty much like early EVP. And note the following. (Things are going to get a little spooky).

'He attributed the voices to a friend who was killed in a car accident several years before.'

We go on a few paragraphs in this very interesting report from Seville and we find,

'The hallucinations occurred in various situations. The most frequent were those in which he could hear the sound of car engines.'

You see what is happening? The sound of car engines is acting as a stimulus for the voices.

Here is the next way in which the auditory hallucinations were stimulated.

'A second [set of stimulators] ... where there was a high probability of hallucinations ... involved those social situations that led to nervousness or anxiety. For example, being in places where there were people he didn't know, and with whom he had to initiate or maintain a conversation, crowded buses, visiting a place for the first time and having to interact with those present, etc. The more anxiety he felt in these situations, the greater were the intensity and frequency of hallucinations.'

And here is an interesting point for us that are into EVP. Here is what Drs Salvador Perona-Garcelán and Carlos Cuevas-Yust have to say about it.

'The lowest rate [of auditory hallucinations] was produced by the third group ("white noise"-like sounds).'

This confirms Alpha findings – white noise has a relatively low Yield compared with Alpha or other modern methods.

There is another interesting correspondence brought out by the following tests – I will only include Trial One and Trial Four – the others gave zero Yield (Utterances per minute). Here is what the doctors say.

'Trial One: the therapist and the patient stood by the traffic lights for five minutes, without speaking. As in the previous trials, the patient snapped his fingers every time he heard a voice. Fourteen hallucinations were reported.'

Trial Four: in the same location, without speaking. Thirteen hallucinations were reported.'

In EVP terms that is almost as good as it gets even with the most sophisticated Alpha system – but with a Yield of 2.8 (or 2.6 in Trial Four) – both EVP and those auditory hallucinations are in the same ball-park, I would expect a yield of 3 for an Alpha current prototype. Their respective Yields are too close not to be regarded as significant.

There is one final correspondence we will pick up on here. It describes the effects of the treatment that may be summarized as frequent exposure to the stimulatory factors while using coping strategies. Here is what the doctors say,

'Immediately after the commencement of the treatment, we observed an increase both in the scores for hallucinations and in those of the psychosis index, probably as a consequence of the exposure treatment carried out, with scores being obtained of 7 points on the former scale and 13 points on the latter.

However, having reached this maximum, there was a gradual and steady decrease of the symptoms, so that by the end of the treatment non-pathological levels were attained in both measures. The more the patient was exposed to the different situations in which it was most probable that auditory hallucinations would occur, the more anxiety towards them decreased.'

Their anxiety was "running-out" – they were getting used to it.

Now, note this,

'[A]nd the characteristics of the voices altered. At first, as mentioned earlier, what was heard were frequent short phrases or words, high in tone and easily identified by the patient.'

I am not entirely certain what they mean by high tone, here – as they didn't hear the voices themselves. I don't think it means high-tone in the sense of being high-pitched, nor does it mean loud, what it means, I believe, is 'Demanding', 'Uppity', 'Domineering' - something like that.

'Later, the frequency, clarity and tone level began to decrease, and an interesting phenomenon relating to the content of the voices was produced.

Originally, they were quite upsetting for the patient, but as he confessed to becoming calmer, they became less offensive and of a more neutral character, being described by the end of the treatment as murmurs or noises of very low intensity that did not affect his life.

For example, he described to us, at an advanced stage of the treatment, that, as he was taking a shower, the voices he heard were simply giving instructions about what he had to do at that moment: "Turn on the tap", "Get the soap", etc..'

The two points to notice are that the voices have become 'good guys' and that they are acting in a command fashion.

Compare that with the following – taken from my original article in 1985 to the UK magazine 'Light'.[3]

'Four main [EVP] speech formats were identified:

---

[3] EVP - Swedenborg and Hallucinatory Voices' by Alexander MacRae, 'Light'

- whistle speech
- whisper speech
- synthetic speech
- natural (voiced) speech.

In terms of frequency of occurrence the order was: -

1.   Whistle

2.   Whisper

3.   Synthetic

4.   Natural.

As the operator used the equipment, over a period of weeks ... the "whistlers" became less frequent, whispers more frequent, and so on, the most frequent format gradually shifting in the direction, "whistle" to "natural" [from 1 to 4.]

Whistle utterances were generally brusque, spat out, dismissive, rejecting or commanding, questioning or suggestive. In some cases the language was sometimes less than temperate.

Similar or identical phrases were picked up by operators quite independently, at different times, in different parts of the country. Examples, "Skip it!" "F . .. off!" "Get away from me!" "Don't do it!"

Whisper speech, [on the other hand,] initially, was typified by voices that somehow conveyed a sense of angelic sweetness, but which seemed vacuous to the point of idiocy. Other cases were less 'nice', "God bless cup of lye", "I got-HIGH!" for example.

With time the whistlers became less frequent, and some of the less palatable phrases occurred during the whispers.

[But]some of the hoarser whispers seemed to have more intelligent content.

Asked what its purpose was, one whisper voice replied, "To guard you."

From an early stage, researchers were cautioned against taking what the voices said by way of advice, or too literally.

Synthetic voices, although relatively infrequent, seemed to give some indication of a desire to communicate ... and possibly of organization, or at least, coordinated activity.

Statements were sometimes made in a way that was disconcertingly factual. A message was asked for a well-known EVP -researcher. The response was "This is the message. . . ." After waiting several minutes for the message which would presumably follow, one was eventually forced to the conclusion that the statement meant exactly what it said, "This is the message"!

Until very recently there was not a sufficient volume of voices of the natural format to be able to spot any definite common factors. Tentatively, though, it would seem that many of the examples of voices in the glottal format ("natural" speech) are concerned with death, heaven, or the name of the speaker.

Interestingly, the energy requirement/complexity of encoding criterion follows the same hierarchical order; whistle speech requiring the least energy intervention traded-off against minimal sufficient encoding for intelligibility; and, at the other end of the hierarchy, voiced speech requiring the most energy 'intervention in order to produce the maximally encoded format.'

The picture that arises from this – and it is similar to what was reported in the Spanish paper above, is that with time there is a gradual shift from "audio-nasties" to more normal, neutral remarks.

What we have noticed with EVP is that there is also a change in the type of voice – from whistle voices, which don't need much energy and are pretty rudimentary in form – towards natural voiced speech – which requires the most energy and which has the most complex format.

Possibly it is something like this that the Spanish researchers meant when they described a shift from high tone to low tone as time went on.

The conclusion is that here is another factor in common between EVP and auditory hallucinations (AH).

Auditory fatigue

There is another source of voices. Anyone can hear voices due to the ear getting fatigued by a loud repeated noise. This is just a mechanical matter – it would seem that the brain is getting so fed up with this loud noise that it starts to shut down the sense of hearing. And so the person seems to go temporarily slightly deaf. They have been "deafened" by the continual bombardment of sound. This means that the sense of hearing – the sound from the ears – is getting shut down. And this enables the sounds from the mind to be heard.

This is like those sensory deprivation tests where you are put in a darkened tank full of liquid where you just float – no sights, no sounds, no pressures – nothing – and during those times people experience very vivid "dreams" without sleep. The noise from the outside senses is shut down, and so the other stuff, the mind sounds – which are always there – has a chance to be heard. So you hear things which have no physical reality but seem just as real – as though they did have physical reality.

And going beyond that, some drumming people – Voodoo, Sufi – make use of this "technology" to affect a sensitized person, so that they appear to be taken over and can speak with the voice of a dead person.

The people generally credited with finding EVP as we know it, were (almost simultaneously), in Sweden, Friedrich Jurgenson, and in the USA, Attila von Szalay.

Friedrich Jurgenson was held in such high regard that he was given a medal by the Pope. It is not clear if this was connected with his EVP discovery.

A recent hour-long documentary on British television in which the present author appears reveals that the Vatican has given its backing to this kind of research – and in fact one of the leading people in EVP is a priest, Professor Francois Brun.

In his talk on the TV show Professor Brun revealed that the first people to receive EVP were in fact two priests working in the Vatican, Father Gemelli and Father Ernetti, who in

Friedrich Jurgenson and Pope Pius

1952 were experimenting with one of the new steel-wire recorders developed by the Germans in World War 2.

The reputed earliest modern case of EVP was in 1905 when messages were received in Morse Code, which should not have been there. Of course there was no way of recording it, then.

But much earlier than all this, according to folk beliefs, there was a tradition of hearing voices near waterfalls.

Waterfalls were considered to be where spirits lived.

Why waterfalls? Well, remember that a waterfall – in sound terms – is an almost perfect source of White Noise. And with a continual loud source of White Noise deafening the ears – eventually voice-like sounds will be heard.

Charles Dickens, in his story, 'The Mystery of Edwin Drood', (1870), wrote,

> "Then, he stood intently listening to the water. A familiar passage in his reading, about airy tongues

which syllable men's names, rose unbidden to his ears.'"

That could be quite a good description of EVP –

'airy tongues which syllable men's names....'

The frequent uttering of names was one of the first things noticed after we started using the Alpha Technology Interface Unit and we began to get voices in abundance. The abundant supply of results meant that we could study and analyze what we found.

We were getting names. Lots of names – the main thing that we got were names. First names, a complete name sometimes – men's names, women's names.

But long before Charles Dickens there was a very strange case in Biblical times.

Without being sacrilegious, and pointing only to *the means of communication*, I would suggest that perhaps the first known case of what we now call EVP, occurred in the time of Moses.

A Biblical Case?

Moses, in the desert; came across a burning bush, and from the burning bush a voice spoke to him.

Once again, without being in any way sacrilegious, I would like to point out that the sound of a burning bush – if you listen in a totally quiet environment – no cars, no radios, no birds – no sound pollution – sounds like random noise. The hissing and the crackling of the burning branches add up to a pretty good random noise source – like White Noise.

And it was from this burning bush that Moses heard the voice of the Lord.

OK – this is not a lesson in religion – any religion – this is about *EVP* – but, just to illustrate the point, Skyelab have repeated the burning bush (actually a clump of heather) – as an experiment to demonstrate that the sounds of a burning bush are a valid source of random noise. And to save any more bushes getting burnt we put the sound on our website! But it should be firmly pointed out that if you use this sound you should carry out the experiment with the utmost respect, and if you hear anything it will not be a repeat of the Moses experience. And as the recording was made in a Skye garden in early summer rather than in a desert you will also be liable to hear quite a lot of birdsong!

The point that I am making is that hearing voices one way or another is not new – so why the sudden upsurge in activity?

What is different about today is that now we have the best technology available to investigate this further. It is all waiting to be discovered.

EVP as we know it saw the light of day with the coming of the tape recorder. The reasons for that are not mysterious. It is possible that people had picked up voices before – they had just heard them, outside, or picked them up on a radio, for example.

But with the coming of generally available tape recorders it was only a matter of time before someone actually taped one of these voices. And there was the proof – preserved for posterity.

It so happened that for Jurgenson the first EVP voice he heard was that of his late mother and she addressed him by his childhood name – "little Friedl". And so it was only a short step from there to assuming that we were somehow contacting the realm of the dead with our recorders.

That is what some people believed – but to me that was shockingly unbelievable! That was how it seemed to me, when I eventually heard about it. I thought it was yet another con, yet another pseudo-scientific con.

Recording dead people speaking – I dont think so! What a cruel joke. Or so I thought.... Years before I had done research for NASA and other agencies on what happens to speech and hearing in difficult circumstances – and if I didn't know all about speech and hearing ... well, who did. So, as a plain fact, and from a real expert in the field, not some pseudo-science con artist ... I would say that EVP was at best someone's delusion, at worst yet another money-making con.

Sensible people do not believe in EVP. I haven't spoken in detail about this before, but three years after encountering EVP for the first time, when working as a lecturer at Lewis Castle College, I happened to invent in my spare time the Alpha Interface System. It was really designed to do something else but it produced voices. The first voice I recorded was that of my late father, and the utterance was also in a kind of code – which few apart from immediate members of the family would recognize.

It didn't even sound like code – but that's the best kind of code – only those who have the ears to hear it, will recognize it.

You can't come up with codes like that, just in a flash – it does take some thought on the part of the speaker of the words.

I also *recognized* the voice – so both in Friedrich Jurgenson's case and my

Lewis Castle College

own first successful experiments – we recognized a parent's voice and we both recognized what was in effect a type of coded signal. The words were just ordinary words – but for one particular person it had a special meaning.

The speaker encodes it – but the only person who can decode it is the person who has that code in their mind. It is a double-lock system. Simple, and works well.

So – that is another thing that EVP is about – survival. I say – about – because EVP itself is just a phenomenon – it has no religion, it takes no sides – it is we, the creatures of this universe of information, that give it its meaning.

OK, in this first part what I intend to cover is just an over-view of what EVP is – we wont get into any details of what is said – or how to do it – that comes later.

EVP consists of voices which appear in recordings and which have no known origin.

The utterances normally are only two seconds long or less, and are normally in the language of the person doing the experiments.

But what *is* EVP, actually – is it a voice like yours or mine – that is real, that a microphone can pick up?

Yes, in most systems what happens is that the sound is picked up by a microphone and the microphone converts the sound waves into electrical waves that can then be recorded. It has physical reality.

This may sound – as the phenomenon is so unbelievable, no sensible person would believe in EVP – as though what may be happening is just that the microphone is picking up stray sounds from somewhere – or possibly, stray radio broadcasts. That would be pretty sensible and reassuring?

Indeed – but what this first part is about is telling you what EVP is – not What EVP is Not – that is coming next....

And here, in this part, what we have been saying is that EVP is definitely a phenomenon with the characteristics mentioned above.

Remember that what you are reading here is coming word for word from one who has spent over 20 years researching EVP, one of the few in EVP who was paid to do research as a profession in speech and hearing, and whose talents were valued enough for him to be recruited to go – all expenses covered – to work under a Secret Clearance on contracts for NASA, USN, and others, in Palo Alto, or as it is more popularly known, Silicon Valley.

It is unlikely that you will have heard of me – especially not with regard to EVP, but the subject is becoming better known, and hopefully one day soon people will be able to research this most exciting field – and make a living doing it.

At present, it is only the royalties on the sales of this book that keep this research going, for me.

EVP and the author's work have been receiving more attention in recent years, however, which is a great and welcome change.

For example an hour-long documentary was shown in the UK, that included the work of most of the leading people in the field.

TV Documentary about EVP in UK

The David Monaghan Productions TV crew at Grianan

In the spring of 2001 while still working on earlier book, down in Calpe, in the Valencia region of Spain I received a phone call from the UK.

This was from a lady producer at the UK's main television network, the BBC.

We then had a long conversation about EVP and what I thought of it. They were planning a program about possible survival after death and the main person involved was someone called Justine.

The BBC people visited Grianan shortly afterwards and really I had nothing set-up to show them, which I am sure didn't help much.

In the end, I was told, Justine decided to not go ahead with the program – something for which I could not blame her.

Shortly after, however, a TV crew from DMP, doing a documentary for the UKs nationwide Channel 4, appeared.

They were on Skye for several days and took shots of the Alpha equipment being used, and analysis of the sounds using sound-editing software.

The local Church of Scotland minister, the Reverend Dr. John Ferguson, was invited to the house and our discussion was filmed. I was interviewed also about George Meek's Spiricom – you will read more about Spiricom later, and I expressed the opinion that the sounds reminded me of the voice in a children's record of the 1940s called 'Sparky's Magic Piano' – in which a piano is made to "talk."

By good research, DMP were able to obtain a copy of 'Sparky's Magic Piano' and that was played during the program.

The TV team moved on to America in July, where Dale Palmer was holding a convention in Fairfield, Indiana. This was held to promote his new computer system for EVP (which will be discussed later) and to promote his triadic philosophy to explain reality and phenomena.

The author was invited along as part of the TV program.

The completed program was shown nationwide on the UK Channel 4, in the 'Witness' series, in December 2002, and judging by the response, was well received.

At the date of writing this, there are rumors about a Hollywood feature film being made, which involves EVP in the plot.

Chapter Two

EVP – What it is not

This is a pretty mystifying phenomenon isn't it – voices from nowhere – there must surely be *some* explanation, some hopefully *rational* explanation.

The mind likes things that make sense. It does not like things that don't make sense.

Here is how Professor Richard Wiseman of the University of Hereford defined EVP on an hours-long nationwide TV program in the UK in 2003. Professor Wiseman is supported by the Perrot-Warwick Scholarship and the Bial Foundation – both bodies dedicated to the investigation of the paranormal.

I have not been able to find any reports of experiments in EVP carried out by Professor Wiseman and he does not reply to my emails. If you have seen the original on TV you will know that with his repeated sales message and the use of body language for emphasis, he is most impressive. Here, you will have to do with the bare words.

Notes:

I am of course open to correction but I think that in what follows when the Professor uses the word 'ambiguous' he may have meant to say 'dubious.'

The professor's use of the word 'static' is somewhat dubious in that there is no such sound as 'static.' The word was used in the past to denote the electromagnetic impulse(s) resulting from electrostatic discharge – such as might result from distant lightning or the operation of machinery. Thus one might find dialog in an old B&W film about a ship during WW ll.

> **Captain:** "We ought to be picking up some French stations by now." Frowns. "Anything on the jolly old wireless, Jock?"
>
> **Jock:** "Nothing, Skipper. We are picking up nothing but static, sir, summer lightning, perhaps..."

As modern equipment is relatively immune to static it is not quite clear as to why the Professor should introduce such dated terminology, and in a not entirely appropriate fashion.

I have no wish to be unfair, nor to rush to judgment, so let my learned "Media Friendly" friend make his point, himself, in this short quote.

The Professor's Message

<u>Professor Wiseman</u>

> 'With electronic voice phenomenon people are listening to noise – to static – and they really want to believe there's some kind of message in there – that spirits are talking to them – and so they're listening out for any hint of a message – and as humans when we look at something ambiguous when we really want to hear or see something in there we're very good at hearing patterns at hearing fragments of words convincing ourselves that, yes indeed the dead are speaking to us when in fact we're just projecting our own wishful thinking onto ambiguous patterns – we're not hearing the voices of the dead – we're hearing static, we're hearing noise, and we're reading meaning into that, we're hearing what we want to hear.'

What a pitch - our Richard could make a fortune on a market stall – but one wonders what the Bial people and the Perrot-Warwick people would make of that! He seems so definite about what he is saying. No gray areas there – he seems so convinced and so convincing. Really getting the message across. And note the skilled use of repetition – to really drive the message home. That is one talented communicator. As we go on we will examine his various points, one by one.

And so people think up all sorts of explanations as to what EVP might be – so long as it is not EVP as I have just defined it. That is *way* too spooky.

But some of the "rational" explanations are actually so far out that you would have to be somewhat suggestible, even "un poco loco," to take them on board.

"Obviously," you may be told, "Obviously, it is the sound of toilets being flushed and the sewers conducting the sound all around the city. Especially in the morning."

That is one explanation

We all seek the conventional in the face of the unknown – this is nothing new – I do it myself.

"What this so-called EVP is," someone will tell you, in the most convincing manner, "Is pick-up. Your microphone picks up stray sounds and because they are so weak and indistinct you think they have an unknown origin and call them 'EVP'. That's all it is. Pick up."

You will soon find that the world is full of experts on the subject of EVP, even if they have never heard it – *especially* if they have never heard it!

Someone else may advise you, "What this so-called EVP is," they will tell you, in the most convincing manner, "Is pick-up. You are picking up bits and pieces of radio broadcasts and because they are so weak and indistinct you think they have an unknown origin and call them 'EVP'. That's all it is. Pick up."

What you are getting here is pseudo-science and anecdotal evidence. The guy – or girl – may have a double Ph.D. in Bio-Chemistry and be a Professor of Animal Genetics but that does not mean that they know anything about EVP – other than the pseudo-science and anecdotal evidence that they in turn heard from someone else.

There is a fundamental problem here. Everyone thinks that EVP is a small pond – and there are an awful lot of people who want to be a big fish in a small pond.

And this goes as much for obscure academics at some little known institution, as for the technician or draftsman who wants to be recognized as an electronics expert. Perhaps it is a sign of an increasing occurrence of Munchhausen's Syndrome[4] in our celeb-driven society.

But EVP is not a small pond – it should be a universal pond – it is the way to put each person in touch with greater aspects – but it has been subject to suppression, misappropriation and fairly crude fraud.

The truth is that anyone who uses it for personal aggrandizement, for gaining control of others, for promoting phony or false and discredited beliefs – that person is standing in the way of Evolution – and that is not a terribly wise place to stand. One is liable to get run-over.

The Spanish Experiment

Real evidence comes from experiments.

I knew EVP wasn't due to stray pick up, but to prove the point what I did was to take the Alpha Technology Interface Unit (AT-IU) – the thing that produces the EVP – to a small town in Spain.

At that time there was nothing on the radio but Spanish stations and most of the speech in the street was in Spanish.

So – EVP was pick-up was it?

That's what they said. OK, then lets switch on the Interface Unit and pick up some Spanish.

I did a session a day, around 10:30 in the morning, for five days.

And the result – not one word of Spanish. Everything was in English.

Now wouldn't you say that was a logical experiment – and wouldn't you say that the logical conclusion must be that whatever EVP is – it isn't pick up – not radio pick up, not microphone pick up, not pick up of any kind? Wouldn't you say that?

---

[4] A desperate need to attract attention to oneself and to try to raise one's public esteem.

Where's the Spanish? Where's the pick-up?

On the basis of technical arguments it had been obvious to me it wasn't pick up. I knew that already – even without going to Spain. But technical arguments you can't explain to everybody. And so I went to Spain. Though it was obvious all along.

It really was so obvious. For example – where was the music? Most broadcast output is music – so the Interface Unit ought to have been producing music if EVP was due to pick up. Instead of words you ought to get mostly music, if it was stray pick up.

Where's the music?

All you got was words.

Words and Communication

And more than that, in EVP each utterance began with the first word of that sentence, and ended with the last word of that sentence.

Now if this was stray pick up, if this was just some random or chance event, then most utterances ought to begin *somewhere in the middle of* a sentence and end s*omewhere in the middle of* another sentence. That is what happens with a random process – there are no rules. Where the beginning is would be purely a matter of chance and where the ending is would also be a matter of chance.

Instead, what we get in reality is – the first word is the proper first word and the last word is the proper last word. And that is not chance – that is not how chance operates. This is no stray pick up of any kind. It has the same format as that of an intentional communication.

You would think that the Spanish experiment would have proved the point – but no – there are still people who dont get it.

Just because someone is against the idea of EVP does not mean that they are *sensible* – it may just look that way. In the real world being sensible just means taking the *safest* course.

Where the big problem lies is this. There are those who have an emotional investment in EVP not being right. What one is running up against is not an intellectual barrier but an emotional barrier. So logic is no answer – you will never get through an emotional barrier with logic. Logical arguments like – 'Where's the Spanish?' or 'Where's the music?' Do not get through.

They will refuse, they will deny, they will walk off – it is almost as though they are somehow threatened, as though you are attacking their identity. Sometimes a person can become so identified with their viewpoint on things – even if originally the viewpoint was that of their dead dad or their professor, and they just adopted it – that anything that is seen as a threat to that viewpoint is seen as a threat to their identity.

And you thought EVP was fun? Dont worry – it is!

But if you find yourself in discussion about EVP with someone who seems to have a very fixed viewpoint about things, or who is getting emotional – then just let it be. EVP is not a religion. Let them, in their own eyes, be right. Its no big deal.

Sometimes this emotional barrier does not arise until the person has heard EVP for the first time. Just occasionally someone will be so startled by finding out that it is *real* that they will go into immediate denial.

This happens. I think it may have happened to me at the very beginning.

The Faraday Cage

There are those who couldn't see the point of the Spanish experiment.

So I carried out another experiment.

You have probably heard of a Faraday Cage? This is a room that is shielded by metal walls so that no radio waves can get into that room. Scientifically, it is used for tests of sensitive equipment and measurements that might be affected by picking up the energy of radio waves.

It is essentially, a room built to prevent radio pick-up.

In the early 1970s a young man called Ellis was doing a degree at Cambridge and he was awarded financial support from something called the Perrot Warwick Scholarship to enable him to research EVP.

It was quite an exciting time in British EVP and there were a few genuinely expert people looking into it.

Ellis traveled to Europe to meet the then EVP expert Dr. Konstantin Raudive. Raudive, it was believed, was able to come up with results on a constant basis.

Dr. Raudive was <u>not</u> a scientist – as many have been led to believe, but a writer and philosopher and so one should not expect too much of his experimental methods. What he *was* however, was a great promoter – so much so that people started to refer to EVP as "Raudive Voices" – which really wasn't fair on Jurgenson - and so the English publisher of his book, Colin Smythe, invented the term Electronic Voice Phenomenon.

Even to this year, more than 30 years on, there is a Hollywood movie coming out called 'White Noise' that attributes the discovery of EVP to Raudive. Here is a short quote from Box Office Prophets,[5]

> 'The next time your radio or television station turns fuzzy and full of static, you might not want to turn it off. According to the premise of the Michael Keaton movie White Noise, it might mean someone's trying to get in touch with you.
>
> The phrase "white noise" itself refers to EVP (Electric Voice Phenomena), an abnormality that is frequently researched by genuine ghost hunters. Discovered by Dr. Konstantin Raudive, a Latvian psychologist who was a student of Carl Jung, such EVPs occur when spirit voices are captured on audiotape. Though such voices are inaudible when they occur in real time, it is possible to hear them on playback levels in a range

---

[5] http://www.boxofficeprophets.com

from 0-300 Hz (live human voice has never been recorded below 300 Hz). Dr. Raudive captured tens of thousands of spirit voices on audiotape, all under very strict laboratory conditions, not to mention the assistance of a physicist and an expert in electronics.'

So – "genuine ghost hunters" – now you know.

(More balls than at the Wimbledon Fortnight.)

Dr. Raudive was multilingual and so it should not surprise us that many of his results were also in different languages. Remember that EVP follows the language of the experimenter. Of course, that principle was not know then, so no one picked up on it.

In fact it sounded like he was picking one word from one language and another from another in order to make the utterance come out as something meaningful. No one suggested that he did it deliberately, to mislead – but perhaps he was a little too enthusiastic about his subject and less critical than he might otherwise have been.

Dr. Raudive became however the "big noise" in EVP at that time and so not only did Ellis go over to Germany to visit him, but he brought Raudive to England to carry out some tests.

One of the people interested in EVP was A.P. Hale. I was surprised by this, as he was one of the top people in electronics research in the UK. He was also high up in the British Institute of Radio Engineers (now the IERE). Engineering Institutions

A. P. Hale

are notoriously conservative, and quite rightly so. The Patron of the Brit. IRE at that time was Lord Louis Mountbatten, cousin of Prince Philip, husband of the Queen of England, and another Board member was the first man to make a direct radio link from England to Australia – and who forecast the coming of EVP in 1929.

Hale worked for a well known company in the UK called Pye Ltd. – and it so happened that Pye had one of those rare items

– a Faraday Cage, that it used for its very sensitive defense work.

The last time in the UK that I had much to do with a Faraday Cage – this was on the Polaris upgrade – well even with that sort of clout we had to book a week-long window, a <u>year</u> in advance!

Ken Attwood

But somehow Hale managed to swing getting the use of the Faraday Cage for EVP experiments with Raudive and Ellis, and the experiment was carried out. The Chief Engineer at Pye at that time was Ken Attwood.

You may have heard that as a result of the Pye experiment 200 engineers heard marvelous results!

Far out – eh? Except that it never happened. Ask the people who were there. Believe me, if 200 engineers had heard marvelous results they would have started experimenting, themselves, or got the company to do it, in this incredible new field, with all its chances for discoveries and entrepreneurship. They would have seized the opportunity.

The present worldwide prosperity is due to the advance of technology – not to politicians and bankers – though they want you to believe otherwise.

And the advances in technology were brought to you by the entrepreneurship of engineers and scientists. We do not let a good chance pass us by.

It is rumors like this one – that 200 engineers witnessed tremendous EVP results in a Faraday Cage – that are so destructive of trying to get the truth of EVP recognized. <u>You cannot build truth out of lies.</u>

The rumor began, so far as I can tell, on a German website, presumably with the best of intentions trying to promote EVP. But you do not promote your subject with untruth.

According to Bander here is what Ken Attwood had to say,

> 'I have done everything in my power to break the
> mystery of the voices without success; the same
> applies to other experts. I suppose we must learn to
> accept them.'

Immediately, I can tell you that this is someone agreeing to a dictated statement.

It is not engineering talk.

> "I have done everything in my power to break the
> mystery of the voices without success."

I don't think so. Media crap.

If it had been,

> "We have not so far been able to determine the source
> of the voices ...."

That would have been believable – that is an engineering statement, but this "*breaking the mystery of the voices*" is sheer book-sellers puffery.

And then there is his use of the word 'expert' as applied to himself. As one of roughly the same generation as Hale and Attwood I can assure you that we would never have applied the word 'expert' in so casual a fashion, and certainly not in respect of oneself.

The first time I came across the use of the word 'expert' in this way was when I first went to the US as a Senior Electronics Engineer at General Dynamics. As I was being introduced around, a balding assistant engineer asked, 'And what are you an expert in?'

For a few seconds I was speechless. I wasn't an 'expert.' To us an expert was some scientist of 50 years experience, and perhaps a Nobel Prize winner, who was called in by the government to advise them on science policy. That was 'an expert.' So I just mumbled 'Nothing, really...' and tried to stop looking so surprised.

But in a few short years what was called "an expert" had changed its meaning markedly. A plumber was a "sanitary" engineer", a salesman a "marketing executive", and the onward and downward flow of BS globules, globalized.

This is what A.P. Hale said about the experiment,

> 'In view of the tests carried out in a screened laboratory at my firm, I can not explain what happened in normal physical terms.'

This has been treated by the True Believers as though Hale had said, 'Well Glory Hallelujah!! Great day in the Morning - a Miracle, a Veritable Miracle, has come upon us!!!!'

In actual fact what Mr. Hale said, in engineer-speak was, as any engineer would tell you,

> ' .' or possibly, ' ....'

In other words,

'Nothing.' (Zilch, nada, rien, niente, x/∞,)

In recent correspondence Ellis has pointed out that both Hale and Attwood in private, to him, expressed their lack of accord with what they were reported as having said about the experiment. Both Bander and Raudive were seeking to promote their respective books.

Here, finally, is what Ellis has to say, [6] and note his deliberate use of the word 'propaganda.'

> 'As this experiment was used for propaganda for "*Breakthrough*" [Raudive's book] and the validity of the voice phenomenon, I expected to hear a number of interesting voice effects on it. Raudive is said to have identified some 200 voice phrases.'

I believe this is where the rumor about the 200 engineers started. It is also a rather extraordinary Yield figure.

The total session time was 9 minutes and 45 seconds, so 200 utterances in that time would have meant an utterance every 2.925 seconds. And as the most probable duration for an EVP utterance is around 1.75 seconds this would mean that the average gap between utterances was only 1.15 seconds.

---

[6] '.The Mediumship of The Tape Recorder' by David Ellis. Fernwood, West Chiltington, Pulborough, West Sussex RH20 2 QT, UK

My own carefully considered view of this is that it is totally unreal – even if Raudive himself believed it.

According to Bander's book the recording was 18 minutes long, but David Ellis has since informed me that the first nine minutes *consisted of the personnel involved with the experiment talking among themselves*. This, I believe, was what the polyglot visitor, Raudive, mistook for EVP voices.

And Mr. Ellis[7], had this to say, (following on from the above, in which he had said that he 'expected to hear a number of interesting voice effects on it'.)

> 'I listened to the ... recording several times ..., but I was quite unable to hear any voices at all – or even any sounds which might in my view be mistaken for voices!'

Remember, this is the same Mr. Ellis who had already heard a lot of EVP. And later, he continues,

> 'On 28th February, Mr. Bearman [8] lent me the tape on which he had recorded the evening's proceedings on his own recorder, and it seemed fairly clear from studying both that the tape I had was the only one made by the Pye engineers.'

So – things were looking a little "murky."

Mr. Ellis now decided to send the tape on to Raymond Cass, the prominent English EVP researcher and hearing aid consultant.

> 'So on 7th March I made a copy of the tape and sent it on to Mr. R..A. Cass for a second opinion.

---

[7] David Ellis. Fernwood, West Chiltington, Pulborough, West Sussex RH20 2 QT, UK

[8] H.V. Bearman, "Breakthrough", an informal discussion in 'Light', Winter 1971, pages 160-166.

Mr. Cass' first reaction was "It .. is itself worthless and negative". When I assured him it was the complete recording ... he listened again.

This time he reported "a quick poor quality voice which seems to say Hugo ... it is by no means the sort of voice that I would offer as evidence of the phenomenon.... If anyone says there are other voices on this tape then it is I who needs a hearing test."'

I am rather more inclined to believe Ellis and the late Raymond Cass – it is really not up to the enthusiasts to expect everyone else to share their enthusiasm *without question*. Unfortunately, there is a lot of that in EVP.

There never were 200 engineers, indeed it is probable that there never were 200 utterances on the tape, either.

But yet this was reported and re-reported and re-re-reported – and it is supposed to be one of the foundations basing EVP firmly in the world of reality. You can't get much more real than - count them - Two Hundred engineers.

So after the time to use the Cage had passed they had found only one utterance, '... a quick poor quality voice which seems to say Hugo ... by no means the sort of voice that [would be offered]as evidence of the phenomenon....'

But – if it was real – one is enough. And this could not possibly be due to stray radio pick up. So had the existence of EVP been proved?

Steady On – Chaps!

Common sense prevailed and they decided that it was a case of picking up sound waves. Somewhere around the Faraday Cage someone must have spoken.

It couldn't have been any of the experiment team because one of the things you do in these experiments is make sure that you do not speak – even inadvertently – during a session.

So – it must have been someone else.

And on that sensible note the Cambridge research was concluded, and EVP was proven to <u>not exist</u>. And I expect the Perrot-Warwick people heaved a sigh of relief.

"V8s all round, chaps!"

And with that, interest from serious researchers anywhere in the English-speaking world was killed off.

Thirty Years Later

I tried to find if I could get the use of a Faraday Cage in the UK, to repeat the Pye experiment. It was a long and disappointing search.

There were some – particularly in my home country, Scotland – who were extremely unhelpful. But then that might have meant someone getting access to the limited funds that were already sewn up for a fixed few. Never make the mistake of assuming that Scotland is not a corrupt country. It is true that a lot of inventions and discoveries have come from Scots – but what is not mentioned is the fact that to get any backing they had to go abroad – even to England. John Logie Baird, the Scot generally credited as the inventor of television, at one point, after he moved to England, and was carrying out his TV experiments, lodged with a fellow Scot – a friend from school.

"Would it not be better," his friend advised, "To have stayed with selling cheese instead of getting involved with these experiments..."

The funny thing was that the people who were most helpful in my search for a Faraday Cage were the people who you would expect to be too busy, and who were recognized as the top people in their specialties. One was Brian Josephson of Cambridge, Nobel Laureate; another was Professor Deborah Delanoy, a parapsychologist with a cross-disciplinary reputation and Professor Russell Stannard, Emeritus Professor of Physics at the Open University.

All credit to these people, who one day may be given the credit they deserve when this becomes an in-subject for the leading edge of technological advance.

It is noteworthy that neither the Koestler Institute person at Edinburgh University whose work was closest to this project, nor anyone at the Scottish Society for Psychical Research even replied to emails.

Difficult though it may be for outsiders to believe – but EVP is seen as a threat in an area where resources are scarce and fought over.

In the end an American contact suggested I get in touch with Dr. Charles Tart, the Transpersonal Psychology leader who lived in the California Bay Area. His is a well-known name in the field of parapsychology – it was he who first started taking a technology-based approach to this field and that was back in 1963.

Unfortunately, Dr. Tart could not help either, but suggested that I contact Dr. Dean Radin at the Institute of Noetics Sciences (IONS) in Petaluma in Northern California. This was another well-known name. I had read of his research when he had been at the Koestler Institute in Edinburgh University where his groundbreaking experiments had led to him being referred to as the Einstein of Parapsychology.

And guess what – Radin had a laboratory shielded against radio waves and also shielded against sound waves! And – they would let me use it!

This was from a guy who was top of his profession and getting 200 emails a day.

So – it is interesting to note that the people who were acknowledged leaders in their respective areas of research – Josephson, Delanoy, Tart and Radin had no problem about helping.

I was so relieved that at last the never-ending quest was over. I had the use of a double shielded room to do the experiment.

So this time if any voices were recorded there were no excuses – they were not pick-up of any kind.

It is unfortunate that as the years progress, instead of advancing EVP with research one is stuck back at the beginning trying to prove the point to people who have opinions otherwise.

And so it was, that it came to pass, that on the 3rd day, of the 3rd month, of the 3rd year, of the 3rd millennium the 3-minute experiment was performed.

(No – I didn't set up the numbers – they just came out that way, apart from the session length. We always do three minute sessions. That makes the time taken afterwards to do analysis, reasonable – and it makes session-to-session comparisons possible.)

The great news is that voices were obtained. They were of sub-standard quality – but that can happen when you are just settling into any kind of *new* set-up.

Now, there could not be any doubt that the voices were not pickup. The doubters are vanquished – forever! Now we can get on with advancing the field! Yes?

Well, no.

The doubters say,

> 'OK – its not pick up. You were right. And thanks for spending your own money to carry out the experiment, but these are not really voices – they just *sound like* voices.'

It is unbelievable. What do they say?

> 'These are not really voices – they just sound like voices'

Can you believe it? The next experiment was designed to test that strange idea.

They are not really voices they just sound like voices

Round about this time I wrote a short piece for the ITC Journal about Skeptics. What I advised in that article was that it was not up to us to have to do all the experiments to suit the Skeptic – we should demand experimental evidence from them to support their assertions.

> 'They are not really voices they just sound like voices.'

Prove it. That's what we should say to them. Prove it.

That is how we should respond to such wild claims. Show me the evidence.

But I wasn't listening to my own advice and decided to carry out the experiment to try to prove our case – that these were indeed voices, and that they were saying something which could be commonly understood.

I decided that the way to do this was to get a panel of listeners to independently judge if there was a voice there or not, and to decide what it said.

One of the first things that you learn in EVP is that there will always be someone who disagrees with you about interpretation....

Imagine something like this happening – you are all enthused with your latest recording, and you have a voice saying, apparently, to you, 'Dying for a diet.'

Then someone comes along and says, "No, it doesn't say, ' Dying for a diet', it says 'Dying for a crap.'"

So, what do you do? What is wrong with EVP when people hear different things – is it just an illusion. This one of the most common objections to EVP, and one that troubles us all, so I am going to spend some time on this – if you don't want to read it all, skip to the next heading, The Experiment.'

The Theory

No. There is nothing wrong with EVP. It happens with all sorts of distorted speech, with a bad phone line or radio link, with the speech of someone who is deaf, in a helium atmosphere, and even with normal speech.

You and I, I assume, can both speak with no problem. But if we were to go totally deaf – so that we could not hear the sound of our own voices, so we were deprived of that feedback, then after a while – a month, two months, our speech would begin to sound a bit odd. It would be a bit difficult to understand.

One question is – OK, we can hear these EVP voices and what they say – but can they themselves *hear* what they are saying?

The reason we should look at that question is that there are certain similarities between some characteristics of EVP speech and research done at the University College London Department of Phonetics and Linguistics into the speech characteristics of profoundly deaf people.

Could it be that the entity that is causing speech to be heard, here, physically – cannot hear the actual sounds, itself? It can make the sounds but it cannot hear them?

More research is called for.

So do not be cynical if different people come up with different interpretations of what an utterance says.

When I worked on speech research one of the test methods we used was to have a list of 20 words read out – one at a time – and for the listeners to guess what each word should be.

The words were all monosyllabic – they each had only one syllable. The word "Dock" would be acceptable for the list, having only one syllable, but the word "Doctor" would not – it has two syllables.

This test is known as a monosyllabic word list test. If there was almost no noise, but just the voice reading the list of words, then you could expect close to 100% accuracy in the responses.

If the level of background noise is the same as the level of the voice then you should get only 50% of the words right and the other 50% wrong.

If the level of noise is such that it is half as much again as the voice, then 25% or less of the words will be correctly guessed.

And finally if the noise level is much greater than the voice then the correctness of responses falls close to zero.

OK – that's with listeners of normal hearing and a good speaker.

But if the listeners were partially deaf, then their scores would be much lower; or if the speaker spoke with an unusual accent, then the scores would be lower; or if the loudspeakers and amplifier introduced distortion into the sound, then the scores also would be much lower.

That is logical, isn't it – if you can't hear the thing properly then your chances of getting it correct are lower.

However, I wasn't satisfied with that. The usual way of doing things was to run the standard monosyllabic word tests, count up the correct scores and in that way to find out if any change that you had made was actually an improvement. Could people understand it better - was it more "intelligible", that was the question.

What I wanted to know was how the errors occurred and why.

Say a word on the list was "Soot" but no one wrote down "soot" in their response. Someone had written "Sit" in their response. And someone else had written "Sat", and four others had written "Seat". On a majority vote "Seat" would be "correct". But each person when they wrote down their response believed that they were correct. And we know that it should actually have been "Soot."

You see, saying what is right and what is wrong is not such an easy matter. Each person wrote down what they heard. And in doing that they were doing what was right. For them it was right. What was originally spoken was another matter.

It was at this point that I developed a theoretical approach that I called 'Confusion Matrices.'

A Matrix is just a way of representing all the things that have a common link. In mathematics a matrix or matrices has a special meaning, but that too comes down to the basic definition I have given above.

So, cutting the crap and getting on with it, in the example above, the vowel sound 'oo' as in soot, was confused with (was interpreted as), 'a' as in sat once, 'i' as in sit once, and 'ea' as in seat four times.

'oo" was confused with 'ea' 50% of the time and 'a' and 'i' 25% of the time each - and, surprise, it was not interpreted as itself at all - so it was "confused" with itself ('oo') 0% of the time.

OK - have you had enough? Do you give in?

Using a theoretical approach like that it was possible to predict how a particular listener would respond in particular circumstances. So remember that just because there are a variety of interpretations it does not mean that there is something fundamentally *wrong* with EVP. It happens all the time, with normal speech, but you need to be in the "biz" to know that.

The Experiment

Interesting point – in the panel listening test, the top listeners – the "Magnificent Seven" – were all *high achievers in their own field.*

To begin with, it is always worthwhile to check one's own hearing against that of others *known to be good.* I knew that I was good at this, after so many hundreds of hours of EVP and listening to distorted speech during research for the Space Program, but it would be better to just check it again.

Listening Panels and Multiple Choice Tests

I selected 30 people from my email list and asked them if they would do a listening test for me, using email. They agreed. I took some EVP samples and for each sample suggested 5 different possible interpretations. Table 1 shows an example of the type of thing.

Next, I sent an email to each of the 30 people. It had an attached audio file that let them listen to the chosen sample for this test. As all the emails were sent as "blind copies" each person thought they were the only one doing the test.

In the email I asked each person to choose which one of the five options was the correct one.

Table 1

	A	B	C
1	Hallo Jasmine	Charge maximum	Lunch tablemate
2	Bottle opener	Favor brown	Board games
3	Simple braced	Regarding Joe	Make deposit
4	Even Edward	Practice faster	Dream Spinners
5	Grim fiction	Daily Delight	Harry Roberts

This how the email went.

'I would be most grateful if you would help in carrying out some EVP research. It will take less than 5 minutes but could help enormously.

On the attached audio file you will hear 3 utterances – listen to them as often as you wish – on headphones if possible – if not just turn up the loudness a little.

Before listening look at the following options (five for each utterance A, B and C). Please let me know which option you think best fits each utterance....

Thus if you think A is 2, B is 4, and C is 1 – then just write A2,B4,C1 in your reply.

Thanks a lot – I need to know if I am on the right lines or if I am wasting my time. Finally, please let me know how difficult you found the test according to the following scale.

D

No problem 9; Very easy 8; Easy 7; Fairly Easy 6;

So-so 5; Fairly difficult 4; Difficult 3; Very difficult 1;

Impossible 0.

So all you need to add to your reply, (say it was, A4, B2, C1) – if you found it Difficult – would be D3.

Just A4, B2, C1, D3.....

Alec'

The person would listen to the sample and then decide which option was the right one. The test was repeated with different samples – and repeated again with still more samples.

What was done was – as shown above, was to send each member of the listening panel an email with an attached audio file. In the text of the email five different optional interpretations to choose from were given – as in Table 1 above.

When they had listened to the audio file and decided which one was the best interpretation they were to email me back. In the end there were 10 who got perfect or near perfect scores – more than I expected, and confirmation that my listening powers were as good as ever! It is interesting to note that three of them did not have English as their mother language, in fact, one found it so difficult, in spite of having a perfect score, that he refused to do any more tests.

I asked the ten top scorers if they would participate in a new set of tests, this time for real, this time for blood, based on the samples recorded in the crucial California experiment. The test was also redesigned – the one shown above being just a trial version.

One listener had found the whole thing so difficult – he was a Spanish speaker – that he declined to join the next test, and two others had to drop out also. So the final panel consisted of seven people – a quite satisfactory number – and remember these were the top hitters in the EVP listening league – the "Magnificent Seven." Their contribution to EVP research is priceless. Once again, it is the busy people, the top achievers, who made time to contribute to the common good.

It is interesting to note that all but two of the panel were professionals – they included two professors, a research physicist and a California Attorney.

From the California experiment I had 10 samples – but the email lines would not be able to handle as much as 10 audio files simultaneously.

So I had to split the experiment into three emails: –

    1)   the first would have three samples,

2) the second email would also have three samples,

3) and the third email would have four samples.

For each sample, as before, we had a list of five possible optional interpretations, similar to Table 1 above, with only one interpretation being right.

Here is a copy of the third email that went out.

Sent: Thursday, April 24, 2003 8:50 PM
Subject: Final test – number 3.

This is the third and final part of the Petaluma experiment voices.

As I have said I am not commenting on any of the results until all the results are in – so if you haven't heard from me – you are not being ignored.

The final part consists of 4 separate utterances separated by short periods of silence.

Here are the instructions -

Listen carefully to an utterance – you can repeat it as often as you like – and then choose from the appropriate table below which option is the best match to the utterance you have just heard.

For each utterance there are 5 possible responses. Choose the one that is the best match to what you heard.

For the first utterance choose from table G, for the second from table H, for utterance 3 choose from table I, and for the 4th utterance choose the best match from table J.

Here are the tables. The sound file is attached as a .wav file.

G

1 Lets move on

2 Sound out Joseph

3 Mummy and Daddy

4 Salt for wound

5 Fold this card

H

1 She's Italian

2 Be a voyager

3 Stay watchful

4 Fan rotating

5 Try emulsion

I

1 What sort

2 Tolerance

3 Thankfully

4 Hiya Mima

5 Weigh-in place

That's all they got. Now, just a test – can you tell just by looking at them – which are the correct interpretations?

Of course *this* isn't a fair test – the actual listening panel members had the *sound* files to listen to – and that *helps*!

The experiment began – and from the beginning it was obvious that the results were going to be interesting.

In fact they were more than interesting, the final results were astonishing! I could not have hoped for such figures. All the listeners were so agreed on what they heard – what the utterances actually said – that the odds against this happening by chance were more than *two billion, billion, billion, billion* to 1!

They knew what they were hearing – and so did I.

Point proven. Home and dry. Sorted. No more crap about *'What you hear are not voices, they just sound like voices.'* How could we ever have given serious attention to such weirdo pseudo-scientific opinions. If you had recorded various people speaking on your home telephone and done the experiment with that – you wouldn't have got significantly better results.

So – here is what EVP is not,

1. It is not pick up of stray sounds.

2. It is not pick up of stray radio transmissions.

3. And it is not just sounds that resemble voices but are not voices.

4. It is not "static" (impulse noise, presumably), and it is not what you expect to hear – it is what it is.

Point proven I think. Yes?

Well, no. The most difficult thing for them to accept is the possibility that there might just be *voices* there.

The Clincher

OK. You remember the listening test with the Magnificent Seven and the ten samples from the California Experiment?

Well, I have to confess – a bit later on I sent out an 11th sample. It was sent as an attached audio file.

Subj: Invitation to test for EVP

> **Date: 19/10/03**
>
> **To: Group**
>
> **File: C:\select\packet2\testfinal.wav (10142 bytes) DL Time (32000 bps): < 1 minute**
>
> **To the good old crew of perfect listeners, and others invited,**
>
> **I would be most obliged if you would participate in one last listening test.**
>
> **It is attached. A .wav file. Choose from,**
>
> 1 **Worrying serious now**
>
> 2 **Drink only after noon**
>
> 3 **Jack Taylor needing boost**
>
> 4 **Take her onset mad today**

5   What song is morning

Much obliged.

AMR

The surprising results are given in the next chapter.

Other Researchers

While I was carrying out my own tests, other experimenters around the world were doing theirs. Below is a picture[9] of the principal speakers at the recent Journal of Instrumental Transcommunication, (JITC), Congress in Vigo, Spain, in April 2004. The group includes several Professors, and others qualified to doctorate level.

Speakers at the JITC Congress April 2004

The speakers included the JITC Director/Editor, Dr. Anabela Cardoso, third from the left, front row;   Professor Ernst Senkowski, research physicist from Mainz, Germany, on her right, and Professor David Fontana, Professor of Psychology at the University of Cardiff, just behind. Papers from the Congress will be covered in the June issue of the JITC.

---

[9] Picture by Carlos Fernandez of the JITC, Calle Carral   23A bajo, 36202, Vigo, Spain

Chapter Three

So how would "the good old crew of perfect listeners" – and others invited – do with this one? It was an especially tricky one – with the emphasis on tricky – but why don't you try it too – just to get the flavor.

Which one – 1, 2, 3, 4, or 5 – would be the correct interpretation?

Here is what some of the listeners thought,

White Noise Control Test Results

From M.

Subj:	Re: Invitation to test for EVP
Date:	25/10/03 03:17:54 AUS Eastern Standard Time
From:	
To:	AVPCO@aol.com

Sent from the Internet (Details)

Alec,

Apparently the voices I mentioned in my previous e-mail were hallucinatory effect caused by prolonged listening to a loud rushing sound like "white noise". This is indicated by the fact that I can't hear them every time I go back to listening to your sound segment (they cannot be repeated on playback).

This effect has already been reported by early Richard K. Sheargold in his booklet "Hints on Receiving the Voice Phenomenon".

In fact what I hear is a short speech like sound (vocalization) at 1.15 sec and a whisper voice (something like "Jack") at 0.5 sec from the

beginning which are reproducible but as I hear it they fit not any of the phrases 1-5.

To conclude in your test final .wav file I do not hear any of 1-5 phrases.

M

From R

Subj:	Re: Invitation to test for EVP
Date:	24/10/03 20:11:06 AUS Eastern Standard Time
To:	AVPCO@aol.com

Sent from the Internet

Alec,

Sorry but I couldn't make something meaningful out of it....

R.

From J

Subj:	Re: Invitation to test for EVP
Date:	20/10/03 07:34:39 AUS Eastern Standard Time
From:	
To:	AVPCO@aol.com

Sent from the Internet (Details)

Sorry, Alec. All I hear is static with rumbling. J

From K

Subj:	Re: Invitation to test for EVP
Date:	26/10/03 05:26:16 AUS Eastern Standard Time
From:	

To: AVPCO@aol.com

Sent from the Internet (Details)

Alex, I can't hear anything on this one. K.

From D

Subj: testfinal.wav

Date: 22/10/03 09:25:38 AUS
Eastern Standard Time

From:

To: avpco@aol.com

Sent from the Internet (Details)

Mr. Macrae:

**Sorry, but I don't hear anything but the hiss
of white noise.**

Have a great day

D.

From JP

Subj: Re: Just your response

Date: 29/10/03 00:16:38 AUS Eastern
Daylight Time

From:

Reply-to:

To:

                mailto:AVPCO@aol.co
m

Sent from the Internet (Details)

Hi,
**I don't know whether I have had a problem
downloading the file but all I hear is white
noise. I have tried through several sets of
good headphones and a nice external amp –
still can't hear a thing above the hiss. Perhaps**

you could **resend it to me (unless I am
missing something).
JP.**

From C

Subj: Re: Reply requested please

Date: 04/11/03 23:29:13 AUS
Eastern Daylight Time

From:

To:

mailto:AVPCO@aol.co
mAVPCO@aol.com

Sent from the Internet (Details)

**Dear Alec,
Herewith my reply regarding the listening test. My
apologies for the delay but I did not want to give up
prematurely and have listened to the recording over
a period of time in order to ensure that I did not
miss something which I could have heard.**

**However, I now have to report that I cannot hear
anything but, as it sounds to me, white noise. Hope
I have not let you down on this one, but I just do
not detect any recognisable uttering. Perhaps it is
old age catching up with me! Greetings, C.**

Here is actual evidence – that is what people said, and
they were not just perfect listeners – among them were
two professors, a lawyer, a Ph.D. – I rest my case.

The difference was that in this case the "speech sample"
was just *White Noise* – of equivalent length and loudness
to the normal speech samples.

And you see what happened – they weren't fooled into
hearing something that wasn't there. They even
apologized for not being able to hear anything. They
thought that there ought to have been something there

– they were <u>under pressure</u> to hear something. But they didn't.

These are honest and accomplished people.

Now if Professor Wiseman and others that thought like him were right, then I ought to be getting emails back from the listeners – ten in this case, including the Magnificent Seven – each one with a *different* interpretation of what they heard. As it was all random, and meaningless, and as they would choose whichever interpretation they wanted to hear, there would be no pattern to it.

It took a long time for everyone to respond. It was getting a bit worrying, but in the end they came through.

I had supplied them with all the excuses to hear illusions – white noise; a protocol they were used to; the expectation of hearing something; five suggested options on what they should hear, as they had done before; the penalty of letting the team down if they could not do it; plus the idea of being a loser or inadequate or getting too old, or all of these.

There was an immense pressure on these previously successful listeners, and high achievers in their own right, to come up with an answer.

The pressure was on to come up with a result – that's why it took so long to get the replies in – and what was the result – zilch – nada – niente – rien – nothing....

Point proven. Home and dry. Sorted. Yes?

Well, no. But we will come to the next objection a bit later on.

In God's name when are we going to have an end to these absurd and unsubstantiated opinions about why EVP is not EVP!

So, what EVP is not,

1. It is not pick up of stray sounds.

2. It is not pick up of stray radio transmissions.

3. It is not just sounds that resemble voices but are not voices.

4. It is not a case of mishearing noise as words that one wants to hear.

What are these people being paid for? Here I am paying for this research out of my state pension – the lowest in Europe – while paid "academics" come out with the most outrageous statements.

Why are they supported – the antagonists with their libraries and secretaries and salaries and career advancement – when we pay for the research out of our own slight resources?

There is no way I will play the victim but listen to this.

Aloha Hey!

Full of excitement and with a sense of achievement that the experiment had finally made the case for EVP I was so happy!

But when I came back from my self-financed trip to California, the first thing I saw – on the newsstand at Glasgow airport – in big black headlines -

Composer will use £30,000 lottery grant to tune into sounds of the dead; Ghostly recordings to form basis of orchestral work:

A prominent Scottish newspaper had a big article describing how a young Scottish composer had been allotted a grant of $50,000+ to compose a piece of music based on EVP.

That was like a kick in the head.

A quote from the article:-

> 'Mr McPherson, from Dundee, will also be traveling to renowned haunted sites around the world for inspiration, collecting electromagnetic readings of haunted sites, and investigating the legends of dead composers ...'

Well, isn't that interesting – especially with Scotland abounding in haunted sites and the leading-edge work in EVP being done in Scotland.

So – where, according to the paper – are the most haunted places in the world?

London, San Jose Northern California, and Long Beach Southern California, Fiji, Singapore, Cape Town, and finally – back in Scotland – the *Royal palace of Glamis*.

Well – well - well – that's quite a travel itinerary isn't it? And it sounds as though the whole thing is going to be filmed!

"Creative Scotland Award" all right. Very creative.

I wonder what electromagnetic readings of haunted sites he will be taking – it doesn't actually say in the article – although it shows pictures of many of the places on the tour. Sounds terribly technical doesn't it? Electromagnetic readings – my word!

So – seeing that – after just spending money I could ill afford on a key experiment in EVP meant that – to say the least – I was not best pleased as I got on the bus for the 5 hour journey back to Skye – where we have lots of haunted sites, incidentally.

I wrote this email to the Editor of the paper concerned.

To: letters@theherald.co.uk

> Dear Sir,
>
> Having just this week returned from a 5-day visit to California to carry out experiments in the Electronic Voice Phenomenon (EVP), it was more than a little galling to read (Herald, 8th March 2003) that a composer is receiving £30, 000 to investigate EVP for possible use in his compositions.
>
> As one who carried out R&D for NASA and other agencies into electronic aspects of speech and hearing and who has supported the research and development of the equipment needed to produce EVP, and who has paid for all this – including the trip to California – out of his own pocket, I am left speechless.
>
> And it is really not on to treat EVP in the same category as "alien abductions" and the like – if you wish to know more about current real-world activity in EVP from those actually working in it, then please

read my paper on the subject in the forthcoming issue of the Journal of the Society for Psychical Research.

Alexander MacRae

Grianan,

Portree,

Skye,

Scotland IV51 9DJ

Tel: 01478612009

AVPCO@aol.com

There was no reply.

I got on with things. As if research in this area was not already difficult enough, having to contend with this sort of thing was the last straw.

Some time afterwards I received an email from my good friends Tom and Alisa at the AAEVP.

They had had an inquiry from a woman representing a TV company in the UK inquiring about EVP.

So they passed her on to me.

The email went as follows,

> Re: Re:Quick chat
>
> Date: 06/06/03 12:03:51 GMT Daylight Time
>
> From: eliya@wagtv.com
>
> To: AVPCO@aol.com
>
> Sent from the Internet (Details)
>
> **I and he would love any contacts – he was trying to get hold of a lady who he thinks is based in Dundee and is involved with EVP, he thinks he saw her on a tv program but I have had no luck finding her for him and he doesn't know her name.**

I think he needs advice about equipment and techniques etc. So anyone who could help him with that would be great.

Thanks for your help!

Eliya

Soooo -he (the composer) needs advice about equipment and techniques etc.

He would love any contacts –

I was unable to help, but could suggest others who might. There was a matter of one's integrity here.

From: <AVPCO@aol.com>

To: <eliya@wagtv.com>

Cc: <david@dumdum.demon.co.uk>

Sent: Friday, June 06, 2003 10:39 AM

Subject: Re:Quick chat

> Hallo Eliya,

> yes I know about Mr MacPherson's "project" – I am afraid though that my stuff, being mainly scientific theories, would not fit in too well with the musical approach – there are lots of others who would be eager to provide suitable material though – would you like some names?

> Good luck – here's an idea – no charge – Big Brother in the Spooky House?

>> Bye,

> Alexander

After a while we heard no more about it. I was told later that they had been advised by a Scottish source that EVP was just a delusion.

And you thought EVP was going to be fun! Dont worry – it is!

Have you noticed something – there were just a few pages about what EVP is – but there are many more pages about what EVP is not.

And this, I am sure is not why you bought this book. So let us now get on to the really important thing – the reason why we have taken so long over what EVP is not is that in an area where resources are scarce (parapsychology), like Madonna's career move you make a career any way you can – and unfortunately some of that means putting EVP researchers down.

In the main EVP researchers are very honest people who do it in their spare time. Some are a bit over-enthusiastic, perhaps not critical enough – but in this field you dont really need to be self-critical – there are plenty others ready to do it for you.

EVP is Just Sounds in Random Noise

There is just one more little piece of pseudo-science that will be trotted out time and again, and I will finish this part and we can get on to the interesting bits.

You have heard that if 35 monkeys were to sit at typewriters and to keep on typing for a billion years – during that time they would have produced the complete works of Shakespeare. Dont worry if you dont believe it, I'm not sure I do, either – its what comes next that is the real pseudo-science.

Using the same argument as the one above where a load of monkeys trying at random will come up with something sensible you will find people who will say that if you listen to white-noise long enough you will eventually hear anything.

Theoretically – that is possible.

But that is not what these pseudo-scientists mean. They come out with this pronouncement, and because they are doctors or professors you believe them. They may be astronomers or experts in Hereford bull genetics or in teaching folk music or the religious beliefs of Amazonian Indians – but that does not mean they know anything at all about White Noise.

They are simply repeating what they heard somebody say. And that, as you now know, is anecdotal knowledge.

You dont have to accept their assertion – ask them for experimental evidence – that is something the pseudo-scientist never has. They are trying to schmooze you with pseudo science.

Ask to see the calculations.

Generally, such people are a bit vague when it comes to math.

Now I am not going to spoil things still further by getting into the math of random noise – just remember this – yes, you could get to hear anything from White Noise eventually – roughly once in every trillion years – and then it might be in Russian or Swahili or any of the 6000 languages on Earth. Not to mention those that belong elsewhere in the universe.

So – does this happen? No. You do not get phrases in Russian or Swahili or Martian or whatever appearing at random - as would be the result with random noise. Instead, hundreds of people, maybe thousands – get EVP results *and understand them.*

Let me just repeat what we have found.

1. EVP is the recording of speech that has no known origin.

2. The utterances are short – typically 2 seconds at the most.

3. The utterances are normally in the language of the experimenter.

What EVP is not,

1. It is not pick up of stray sounds.

2. It is not pick up of stray radio transmissions.

3. It is not just sounds that resemble voices but are not voices.

4. It is not a case of mishearing noise as words one wants to hear.

5. It is not generated by random noise variations with time.

You know we have the evidence for these points, and we have the best evidence – experimental evidence.

EVP has an experimental basis. It is based on mensuration – measuring things, counting things – a numerical basis. It has its roots firmly in the foundations of science.

It is also replicable. I used Alpha Technology. You can use any other workable method you want. Measure times, note languages, find a Faraday Cage....

There is nothing wrong with being a skeptic – I was one once and I am proud of that. Perhaps you are one now. No problem. I wasn't totally convinced until I had produced results myself.

But I am now drawing a line under this.

I have spent *years* going backwards to placate the whims of anyone who offered an opinion contrary to mine. While others were securely ensconced with their salaries and secretaries and libraries and funding from various Foundations, I have spent my own money in carrying out experiments – even traveling 12,000 miles to carry out one – so THAT IS IT. No more.

Except like the monster in Terminator the Adversary keeps coming back to life. Why didn't you use the "musical bubbles" instead of white noise, asked one prominent researcher – "musical bubbles" is the term for a side-effect you get when Noise Reduction is used to improve intelligibility.

So I repeated the white noise test with musical bubbles instead, treating it as though it was a real test, with five options to choose from. I even sent an email with the test to the prominent researcher who had suggested it. As before, everybody was so apologetic for not being able to come up with anything. There was one person who didn't reply – and that was the prominent researcher.

If someone has an opinion to offer then they should offer it with experimental evidence – no pseudo science, no ambiguous statements, no anecdotal evidence.

Research into EVP has been held up for years by the unsupported public statements of reputed Authorities. The only authorities are those who do it. Now, lets get down to earth and common sense and look at the less than simple question of survival. Are these the voices of dead people?

Chapter Four

EVP – The Four Survivors

Survival

Does EVP have anything to say about survival? Is there an afterlife?

From the beginning with Friedrich Jurgenson in Sweden and Attila von Szalay in the US, EVP has been intimately associated with White Noise and with survival after death.

There are those who are rather carried away by their enthusiasm – which is fine – but they get very uncritical about what they hear – which is not.

Earlier I mentioned two examples,

A. One was where the Swede Friedrich Jurgenson heard his late mother's voice address him by his childhood name. The key to that code was in his head. And you can still hear that recording to this day.

B. The second example was where the first EVP I ever recorded using Alpha Technology was my late father's voice saying something that only a person who knew him very well, would recognize. The key to that code was in my head. And that sample, by a miracle, still survives.

You will hear many people say – of course there is an afterlife – listen to the voices – that is what they are – the voices of the dead.

OK – that is what these good people believe.

What we have found is that you need to be very careful about what you hear – that these voices can come from other sources that are not necessarily good guys – sources that can set up little groups to deceive people, little nests of the deceived and send them – in the view of the rest of the world, "raving mad" – loopy, loony.

We will deal with these other sources and their effects in a later chapter.

What we are looking at now is the question of survival after death – of passing on into another life.

This is not a new belief – it is not a New Age phenomenon and it didn't start with the Fox sisters.

The Fox sisters, three young girls who lived in Up-state New York in the 1800s, began spirit rapping, just for amusement in 1848.

Then to their surprise they found that they were apparently in communication with a spirit called Charles Haynes. The spirit told them that he had been murdered and his body buried in the basement of the house where they then lived. Just like

today the young girls were suitably spooked!

They were even more startled when bones were found in their basement!

And from these sensational beginnings the practice of spiritualism expanded explosively.

Margaretta Fox

So much so that the sisters came under attack – not from a mysterious conspiracy of scientists but by the usual suspects. It all sounds so sadly familiar – after 150 years not much has changed.

Kate Fox

Because of their spiritualist activities, the Fox sisters were condemned and attacked by religious fanatics in their own community. They were even besieged by a hostile mob on occasion.

Another thing that rings true – they were even betrayed for money by a relative. Their sister Leah took the money they had gained for their spiritual counseling services.

Leading spiritualists in the United States decided that it was time to undertake an official investigation, asking Congress to appoint a scientific commission to investigate the perplexing paranormal phenomenon that had been witnessed by so many people.

The petition was given by the former governor of Wisconsin, Nathaniel Tallmadge, to Senator James Shields to be presented before Congress.

However, their trust in Shields was misplaced. What he said has a rather familiar ring to it, even 150 years on,

> 'The prevalence of this delusion at this age of the world, [*evidently they thought they were then at the peak of modernity – just as we do now*] among any considerable portion of our citizens, must originate, in my opinion, in a defective system of education, or in a partial derangement of the mental faculties, produced by a diseased condition of the physical organization. I cannot, therefore, believe that it prevails to the extent indicated in this petition.'

You see – it was all down to body diseases.

Here is the response to that slur by a spiritualist called Eliab Capron,

> 'The carpenters and fishermen of this world are the ones to investigate new truths, and make senates and crowns believe and respect them. It is in vain to look for the reception or respect of new truths by men in high places.'

Notice in 'carpenters and fishermen' a reference to Christianity.

We should not forget that it was Christianity that first brought out the idea of an afterlife in the face of fierce opposition.

However, it was not alone. The European pagans in the Celtic area believed in a paradise called Tir Nan Og – the Land of Youth – making the shrewd observation that no matter what Paradise offers, if you haven't got the youthfulness to enjoy it, it is worthless.

Indeed the belief in an afterlife was much more common than disbelief in an afterlife, around the world. Belief in an afterlife decayed in the last Century not due to a Scientific conspiracy but because being preached at is not the best way of communicating to people who are used to being consulted and to forming their own opinions.

The churches did, and still do – a Monsanto[10] on their congregations.

People don't like being preached at – particularly where the preacher may be less moral and less knowledgeable than the people he is telling what to do and not to do. More baloney from another phony.

That is what destroyed the interest in the afterlife.

But people intuitively felt that this physical existence was not all there was to things.

And so they sought this "other reality" in alternative ways – in Zen, in Scientology, in LSD, in Shamanism, in Sufi, in New Age movements, in drugs, in Gurus, in therapy, in lifestyle consultants and personal trainers – its all the same quest.

I was fortunate to be in The City right then – in the years when everybody stepped off the highway leading straight to everlasting nowhere.

It was then too that I got into doing research for NASA in the area of speech and hearing.

---

[10] The reason that GM products are banned in Europe is that Monsanto Chemicals – doing the Runsfeld Hustle – decided that Europe was going to have GM products whether they wanted to or not, and by any means necessary, particularly lies and deception.

In this age, people do not take too kindly to that.

It all came in very useful when EVP came up.

And that is why finding for myself the proof that there is something else was such a liberating experience.

Reading about it is fine – but sometime give yourself the reward you want – by discovering the truth for yourself.

With Alpha Technology we get lots and lots of voices and yet, in all that time there have only been a few cases which proved the truth of survival without any need to believe.

I have given the first two, the Jurgenson case, and my own case – both involving a code residing in the memory of the listener.

There are two more – I call them all The Four Survivors.

Here is number three.

I was about to leave on my way to London to demonstrate the Interface Unit to a Dr. Berger and his wife, the heads of a Florida Survival Research Foundation, when a letter was received asking if I would demonstrate the system to two Scottish physicists – Mike Scott B.Sc. and Archie MacDonald B.Sc..

We agreed to meet in a Glasgow hotel on my way back from London. The hotel was not the best place for a demo as the fluorescent lights interfered with the radio.

To begin with, I demonstrated the Interface Unit (IU) to Archie and Mike and Mike's girlfriend.

Everything went OK. You just "doodled" with your fingers, on the hand-plates, like "automatic writing", unthinking.

Then Mike demonstrated that he could make the thing "sing" without actually touching it. Talent!

His girlfriend did well – but in the normal manner.

Finally Archie stepped up to the IU. Put his hands on the plates – and there was a profusion of speech sounds – we were most impressed.

Then Archie spoke, "What do I have to do to make this thing work?" he asked. The sounds stopped.

The rest of us fell about laughing.

It was a classic illustration of the fact that for this and many other psychic events to happen some "indirection" seems to help.

One moves one's fingers on the handplate in a random kind of way – without thinking – like automatic writing – not trying to control anything – and the voices come through.

So this was what was happening with Archie. The minute he started to deliberately try to make the thing speak – it stopped!

Of course he knew this principle already – being a well-studied man, but had not quite expected it here.

Afterwards Archie said he had heard, on playback, his wife's voice and it was evident that he still had very strong feelings for her, as he described Margaret to me, and how much Margaret had meant to him, and the times that they had had together.

In spite of the rush, the unfamiliar environment and the interference from the hotels fluorescent lights it was quite a successful demo.

Some months later Archie phoned to say how much this session had meant to him. It had kept him going in the lonely months after his wife's death.

That was nice to hear.

He was so impressed that he had fixed up a meeting with a director of one of Scotland's largest electronics companies and wanted me to demonstrate the Interface Unit to them.

What a great opportunity – if they would only listen.

The demo was done in their boardroom, and the IU was laid out on the polished boardroom table. As well as the Director, Mike and Archie were also there.

Shoot – I had forgotten to bring the power supply! Without it there was no show – no demo.

Not a good beginning – but one of their own engineers brought a supply up from their lab and stayed around to listen. I think he may have scratched the table surface as he pushed it over.

Oh dear, dear.

But we switched on and carried out a short session. Then the tape was played back and we came to a point where we heard an elderly lady's voice calling out 'Stephen!' [I have changed the name].

At this point the young engineer, whose name was Stephen, went bright red and fled from the room. Archie, Mike and I all noticed it, but we affected not to have seen anything.

At the end of the playback, to my great embarrassment, Archie, as before, said he had heard his wife's voice.

I promised to copy it out for him when I got home.

Nothing came of the introduction, as I expected, except that if we wanted to have a supplier for the printed circuits we used, then they would be happy to do so.

Back at the lab, the tape was run through, and yes, there was a message for Archie – but it was from someone called Molly.

So, it was with regret that I had to phone him up and tell him that there was a message for him, but regretfully it was not from his wife but from someone called Molly.

"Yes," he said happily, "That's my wife."

"But you told me her name was Margaret.... Over and over again, you told me her name was *Margaret*!"

"Yes, that was her name – *Margaret* – but Molly was the pet-name I had for her...."

Beautifully coded. Molly for Margaret – and only Archie knew the key.

He heard the voice. I did the analysis. *I* told *him* about Molly – but the key was in *his* head. Once again – a double locked message from beyond.

To me these examples represent the best proof. No one is saying,

> "Hallo – Peter? Its lovely up here in Heaven – how is it down there with you?'

Proof does not depend on having to believe anyone.

Unfortunately the tape of that one may have been lost or destroyed.

There is one more – and fortunately the tape of this one has survived – although in poor condition.

The way that this one came about was as follows. A group called Gaia was visiting Scotland and wished to see the IU in operation.

The demonstration took place in the Palace Hotel in Inverness one summer evening in 1986. There were around 20 people present. The use of the IU was demonstrated and then everyone was invited to try a session.

At a fairly early point a lady held up her arm and said she had heard her brother's voice. This was Professor Leslie Williams of New York. I promised that when I got back home to the lab I would copy off that section and send it to her.

It wasn't easy to pick up – these were the days before sound editors. All I had was the recorder with Cue and Review buttons. You needed good ears.

What it said – almost like a voice telegram,

'Leslie... This is it. David.'

David was the name of her late brother, and by very careful listening I noticed that what he said was not "Leslie" – but "Lezzillee" – a three syllable word.

"God bless your good ears, Alec," said Professor Williams, "'Lezzillee' was my family name as a child – it was what the family used to call me as a little girl."

So – the message addressed her by name, it said it came from her dead brother, whose name was actually David, and it used her pet-name – which no one else in the room knew.

She had first heard the message, I had analyzed it and it was I who had come up with the words of the message.

So that is real experimental evidence – fortunately – almost miraculously, the tape still survives. This is evidence that doesn't depend on anyone's opinion. – either for or against.

In each case there was a special key, known only to that person's family members. And that is as good as any evidence that has come via EVP of an afterlife.

Of course there are lots more indications – people giving their names – why? People talking about Heaven – why? People calling out for help – why?

These are good clues – and we will discuss them in detail later on – but they are not proof.

The proof lies in the four coded messages. Hopefully, with time, we will get more.

But even that may not be needed – as you will find when we come to discuss the future of Alpha Technology.

In the meantime we must continue our quest for more knowledge as best we can.

The author and a prominent psychological researcher have suggested a two-year study to investigate if there is actually any link between what the user of the EVP system says and the voices that they hear. In other words, if you say, 'What is your name,' and within twenty seconds there is a voice which says, 'John Smith' then we could count that as a response. The whole thing will be done on a statistical basis, because you can't take one instance ("John Smith") as proof - it might just have been a co-incidence. So I will be doing around 100 sessions and the results will be loaded into a database being operated by an independent company, and what we will be looking for are two things - is there a link between what the user says and the voices recorded in terms of context - are they talking about the same thing, could the phrase be interpreted as a response to what the user said. And is there any sort of link showing up in the timing of the voices heard and what the operator said.

This project has been submitted to the Bial Foundation of Portugal who every few years have invited proposals for research, in the round just past it was for research into the paranormal. There is no guarantee we will get the funding.

Another way to get to the "Other Side"?

During the 'Witness' TV program – the author rows to a special spot – the waterfall, below – in the search for voices. This unusual procedure was suggested by the Producer, David Monaghan, and thus became 'The Monaghan Experiment'. Despite being buried deep in noise – voices were found.

Filming at the 'Bridal Veil' waterfall on Skye.

David Monaghan is in the foreground, the author is on the right.

Chapter Five

The Legion et al

According to some of the original researchers into EVP everything to be heard on EVP seemed to be all sweetness and light, and voices from Heaven – "wish you were here" – spoken postcards.

Utterances would even get twisted so as to mean what the most important person present wanted to hear. I remember one voice from a session that had been broadcast by Radio Luxembourg. The people being interviewed were a group of German experimenters. During the session an EVP voice was heard to say, 'Man's greatest sin'.

One of the important people supervising this session declared – "Man's greatest sin – yes – that refers to the killing of the whales. That is Man's greatest sin."

I thought at the time that Man's ever-present willingness to condemn his fellow Man might also be considered as Man's greatest sin.

From an early stage it was clear that all the Good Guys stuff was not the whole story and that there was a preaching operation going on. There were those who wanted to convince you that they were – pretty much – in touch with Heaven. There are people in this business who see it as a route to getting to be a guru.

For me, in the beginning, there wasn't much sweetness and light in what I heard. At first I did not believe it could be EVP.

It had to be pick up of CB Breakers – of illegal radio of some sort – for these voices were ugly and used coarse language. That was *not* how the books said it should be.

The voices were abusive, commanding, spitting out words, hostile -

"Wouldn't you like to be evil?" coaxed one, in a quiet little high-pitched sinister voice, with a curl at the end of the utterance – making "evil" sound like "eve-vell."

"Wouldn' you like to be eve-vell?"

On another occasion, much in the way that we might say, in exasperation, "Go to Hell!" a high-pitched little voice with a curl in its tail, snapped, **"Go to Heaven!"**

All of the EVP wasn't like this – it was a minor phenomenon – but it was worth noting because no one else had mentioned it.

Mind you – with the Alpha Technology IU we were getting voices in a profusion unmatched since Raudive – and by all accounts many of Raudive's voices were suspect. So, with that huge volume of results, we were more likely to spot things that other might have missed.

One of the most interesting findings in this area was made by a lady, now deceased, called Barbara Jennison.

Barbara was very much a self-starter, which was fine, except that sometimes it made it difficult for her to follow a planned program of research.

I would have a particular approach I wanted us to concentrate on, and then Barbara – who worked from home – would suddenly get a brilliant idea and go off on some unplanned activities.

One of her interests at the time I am writing about was *chakras* – these, according to Yoga teachings, are regions of the body – energy centers.

It happened that instead of following the research plan, Barbara decided to dispense with connections to the hands, and to try connecting to the chakra regions instead.

Yikes!!!

If she hadn't been such a good researcher I would have been quite annoyed. She did have one problem, though. Her hearing was not too good and so she used to send her session tapes on to me to analyze and confirm where possible.

On one of these "chakra" tapes I heard something that I thought important enough to phone her up about.

At this time we were getting lots and lots of names and in fact used to ask 'What is your name?' as matter of course.

So, on the session tape you hear Barbara asking, **'What is your name?'** and a voice saying **'Region.'** This is good I thought – there she is testing these various regions and that is exactly what it says, Region. A little victory!

I phoned her up with the good news. You are dealing with regions and what response do you get – Region!

Her reaction was unexpected. "No – Alec – listen to it again – please – I think we've cracked it!'

I listened to it again.

So, on the session tape you hear Barbara asking, **'What is your name?'** and a voice says – 'Region?' ... is it "Region"? This time I realize that no it is not 'Region' – it is **'Legion.'**

Barbara asks, **'What is your name?'** and the voice says....**'Legion.'** Got it.

I phone up again, 'You ask – what is your name – and it says, Legion'.

'Exactly! Don't you see the connection? Read your Bible.....Alec.'

> **St. Mark, Chapter 5, verses 8 and 9.**
>
> For he said unto him, **Come out of the man, thou unclean spirit.**
>
> And he asked him, **What is thy name?**
>
> And he answered him saying, **My name is Legion: for we are many.**

Well done Barbara – she died a few years ago but her contribution to this work will be remembered.

The Fox sisters – remember – who started all the spiritualism business – something got at them. People around them got all stirred up and attacked them. Their sister stole their money – what had gotten into her to make her do such a thing?

The sisters became addicted to alcohol – another way people are brought low.

A journalist paid them money if they would claim that their experiences had been frauds all along. They did. The media got their story. The sisters got pissed.

The left that sees no right, the right that sees no left, the shadow that sees no light, the light that sees no shadow – all are unbalanced viewpoints. To see reality one sees both shadow and light, for it is out of these, both, that reality is made.

From the Buddha and Jesus on, taking the balanced view has been the path to peace and sanity.

Yes – it looks as though there are pestilential entities that will get a foothold if they can. They may not have any physical existence – they are what I would call denizens of the informational universe.

But among other denizens of the informational universe are beneficent beings – I suppose that Saints would come into that category – and ourselves. We live information, we eat information, we are surrounded by information – and when the physical body dies information carries on.

The informational universe is our "Home" – we will get into that deeper, later.

Just as a furry animal (say) is likely to be carrying around parasites in its fur, or on its skin – like a dog carrying ticks – or in the stomach or intestines like worms in a dog; or bugs like the digesting bacteria in a cow's first stomach (they have four) – so too we can be affected by informational parasites.

The first possibilities of this appeared early on in the IU based research in just a very simple way.

The session had gone a bit flat, not much was happening, it went on and on and then, for no particular reason I decided to switch off. So I gave the usual warning –

'I will be ending the session in one minute",

and, incidentally, that was found to be a good way of stimulating some final voices.

"I will be switching off in one minute – one minute."

One minute later I switched off the IU.

Playback time.

In analyzing the playback various utterances were picked up and decisions made to copy them for archiving or not. Then the long silent period. Then there was a sort of "burp" and just after that you could hear me saying, **"I will be switching off in one minute – one minute."**

So – was that short, dull, voice-like sound – some sort of forewarning – was it the sound of me having just made a decision, and then implementing it?

I could not say – looking back on it I had just decided to switch off on impulse – in fact, to be honest, I hadn't actually decided to go ahead and switch off – I just did it – on impulse.

So was this "impulse" the sound that preceded the action?

Was it possible that a decision could seem to be mine but was actually made by some other mechanism.

There was another instance of the command power of the voices. One of the first voices recorded spat out the following as though a military command, "Don't do it Jack Do it"

And the truth was Jack was a chronic "ditherer" – he couldn't make up his mind, he kept changing his mind. So was that voice exercising a command value over him?

Certainly the next example seems to suggest that sort of thing could occur.

My lead engineer was someone I will refer to as Simon. Simon had a degree in electronics but seemed to have one little flaw. Bright though he was, sometimes if you asked him a question he would just go red in the face, fall silent, and stare at the desk in front of him – looking, unaccountably, quite stupid – which he wasn't.

I never told Simon about EVP but he knew about Alpha Technology and how it could produce voices.

During some experiments he had been asked to make a tape using the IU. He did that – believing these were experiments with some new kind of speech-synthesizer. He was asked to listen to the playback of the tape and when he thought he heard a voce to hold up his hand.

The tape replay was started and then a minute or two later he held up a hand. That piece of tape was replayed a few times and he was asked what the voice said. He looked down, went red and muttered, 'You are stupid.'

Was this voice acting as a command to freeze up his thinking and make him look stupid?

Commands – spooky or what?

Unbelievable?

OK – would you be willing to try just a simple little experiment? *(Heh heh heh........)*

I will assume so.

Get up and walk to the nearest wall and back again.

Who asked you to do that? I did – the "command" came from me.

But who told your legs how to walk?

I didn't. You didn't. There were "commands" that told your individual legs and feet and toe muscles what to do and when to do it – but it wasn't me and it wasn't you.

Subconscious commands. We need them. But sometimes there can be problems.

Remember the book that was written, just about the time that EVP was discovered, by the young lady called Barbra O'Brien – 'Operators and Things'.

Barbra had schizophrenia and she came to the conclusion that we share this planet with other beings – beings without substance – just pure information – but they could affect us. These were the 'Operators' of the title. And we, who were also informational beings, but who had substance (bodies) were regarded by the Operators as 'Things'.

What the Operators did was play point-scoring games. If one Operator was to get his Thing all stirred up against another Operator's Thing, to the extent that he could get one or both of them to emote – then he would score so many points. Of course *if* it went so far that one of them killed the other, or committed suicide – Mega-points!

It's rather like the news interviewers in modern degenerate TV. 'So – how did you feel when you first heard that the dog had killed your baby and eaten most of it. What were your feelings?'

If they can get someone sobbing on camera that is *paydirt* – that is gold! That – and not news content, is what they are looking for. They believe that what you want to see, what you crave seeing, like some kind of vampire, is someone emoting heavily.

This is what careers are made out of – this is what sends pretty girls out all over the world with a camera crew to get the emotion – and if you can't get that then to try to rekindle it by asking, 'How did you first feel when....?'

This is the age we live in. Emoting on camera – ratings soar. Sponsors love that, money pours in. Hallellujah. Great day in the evening.

Weakened by drugs or alcohol, lacking centeredness by growing up with instability, schizophrenia is encouraged.

Acting on impulse – which can be indicative of criminal tendencies – is an easy route for an informational parasite (ip) to control things – to become 'Operators'.

There is nothing easier than for an ip to slip in a quick, "must-do", self-destructive impulse.

Where do impulses come from? Nowhere, of course – they are "spontaneous."

Ah yes. Impulses from nowhere.

This is not to say that all one does must be cautious, careful, planned – for that too can come from informational parasites instilling ideas of disasters. It is fine to follow one's dream and if necessary to go through thick and thin to do so – no matter what common sense might otherwise dictate. All one can do is "lose"!

And you thought EVP was fun? Don't worry – it is!

Even carefully thought-out schemes often end in disaster. As the Scotch poet "Rabbi Burns" put it, in his poem, Ode to a Mouse, 'The best laid plans o' mice and men, gang aft agley.'

And often, on reflection, we find that the best things that happened in one's life happened by accident.

This may not seem to have had much to do with EVP – but it does – and it should be made more widely known.

People who have had nervous or mental or problems should avoid doing EVP experiments – just as one would not recommend that untrained persons should try experiments in deep-diving.

In the future one would hope that EVP experiments will be done more on a *group* basis – leaving the analysis of the results to the most expert member(s) of the group.

For the present it is enough to be aware that the simplistic idea that the only things around are ghosts and us is just not true.

Who said that ETs had to have meat (biological) bodies just like us? Who said they had to have bodies at all? Who said that ETs use slow old, clumsy, klunky, electromagnetic waves to communicate? Does it make sense to communicate using waves that take *years* to reach their destination?

"We is the twentyuff senchurry and we is mega-advanced, right?"[11] Duuuhh.... I don't think so.

I am just using ETs and our own culture-bound ideas as examples, here, to illustrate the point that maybe there is more to learn, for all of us – "Genuine ghost hunters" – and fake ones, alike.

It is our Century and our Culture.

---

[11] Page 33, re Box Office Prophets definition of EVP.

Chapter Six

Trial and Justice

The voice, by the sound of it, was upper middle class, an educated woman, brisk and efficient – the perfect PA. She might have been, one could suppose, an angel.

She spoke in the most matter-of-fact tones – as though she had just looked around my office door to say, "Call IBM." Instead what she said was,

"Call Heaven,"

So – you see the problem we have.

No one is going to believe this.

People stuck in the safe old ideas of yesterday will heave a sigh of satisfaction,

'Aaaaaah – he is mad, quite quite mad – I knew it from the moment I read the first page. Well, that's a relief … now we dont have to take on – what do they call that stuff – unsafe thinking – new ideas?'

And media vampires will crow screechingly *"Blood! Blood!"* as though a dead maiden had just been found, but – even better than that, they will ask,

' How did you feel when you first read that he (68) had an angel secretary (57) who sat on his knee and went through a form of marriage in Barbados, with a Voodoo priest (41)? Must have made you pretty incredulous – shocked I expect -can you recall just how shocked you were right then, at the beginning… really frightened?'

All I did was to carry out a session as usual, as normal, nothing different – except for the new technology, (which I will touch on in a later chapter.) And this was one of the things that came up.

"Call Heaven."

It is just a fact. I am not trying to make a case for anything. Should I just hide it, say nothing about it. Pretend it never happened? Here I am trying to present the truth about EVP and this happens. It does not help at all.

"Call Heaven."

It is just a fact. It happened – and who is to say it was addressed to me, anyway?

Fortunately the recording of this example we still have – so you can make up your own mind about it.

"Call Heaven," indeed. Well ... its only research isn't it?

So ... some time later I decided to treat it as though it *was* addressed to me – and did what the message recommended. "This is me – I'm calling Heaven, calling Heaven".

Yes, I know its crazy; I am certifiable just to do it – just to even think of doing it. But its only rock and roll – or, as we call it in the trade – research. And I like it.

"This is me – I'm calling Heaven, calling Heaven."

The results were not what I expected or wanted.

It was as though some smooth talking lawyer with a curl in his voice had got in on my call, and assumed it was some kind of petitioning – that I was trying to assert my innocence or something. What the voice said was, **'How much for a jury?'** – 'jury' being prolonged and twisted in the tail as though 'Joo..Raay.'

 In a sly wheedling voice, 'How much for a joo-ray?'

All I did was call Heaven as requested, and now there is talk of a Jury.

(And now I am waiting for the white van to come and take me to the Happy Acres Rest Home.)

All joking aside, the word Heaven crops up with unusual frequency in EVP.

And it would seem that some of the voices are having problems.

"Justice!" (Pronounced "Joostice!") cries one in a Northern England accent.

"We are all banned!" exclaims a male voice in a Northern Irish accent. **"Sean is not an enemy!"** protests another Irish voice. The third voice says, **'Deep Seven'** – as though perhaps this was some level or penalty.

A note in passing, the Pope excommunicated members of the Irish terrorist organization.

Peter Bander, (Dr Peter Bander van Duren, who died in April 2004, author of 'Orders of Knighthood and of Merit'), in his splendid book 'Carry in Talking' – now out-of-print, alas, showed that the Roman Catholic Church was then very interested in EVP.

The above sample was a recent recording.

Peter Bander-van Duren with Archbishop H.E. Cardinale

Here are some from years ago, using the basic IU system and selected out because they seemed relevant to what we are discussing here.

They are reproduced from my previous book, unfortunately it is unlikely that any of the recordings still survive.

They did not all occur at the same time – they were recorded among many other things over a six month period, and they do not reflect my own view of things. I was as startled as you may be.

♦ **Save me someone.**

♦ **God deserts me. My hands are so bloody.**

- I'm lying in the boneyard.

- God help me. It's my big mistake.

- Donovan – join us. Today.

- Pity ha ha. He died of a spirit. Help me God. Help me God. That's all oh God."

- Help me. Donovan.

- Hector flee from Horace."

- Help me. Help me up to Heaven.

- Help is a blind pocket.

- I want justice.

- We are all barred or evicted here.

- I'm up to this fire place {Fireplace? Far place?}

- Oh God help me. Please to help me.

- Ted Sullivan. I have 90 day.

- I am a victim.

- Death's a shoot-up.

- Aah – Jimmy Pierce here. We're all desperate.

- Save me – from them – I'm a Christian!

Notes:

i. Note that the words Banned, Barred and Evicted have all appeared, as have mentions of Justice or requiring upward assistance. However, being a victim or not getting justice is a common expressions among criminals – "Yeah well, I was fitted up – wasn't I?' – that sort of thing.

ii. The boneyard is an old dialect word for a cemetery.

iii. Donovan is a folk-singer – now in semi-retirement. Whether this refers to him or not I really dont know. Certainly in the Sixties there were those who "worshipped" him, as they did Dylan.

iv.   Shoot-up could be a drug-user's term; shoot-out is the more usual term for a gunfight.

v.   Hector and Horace are both references to Classical Greek.

vi.   I dont know who Jimmy Pierce is.

vii.   I knew a Ted Sullivan – I don't understand the reference.

Using a new method that favors inter-voice communication here are a few more recent ones.

♦   **God save Mary!** (Distressed female voice – maybe she is Mary.)

♦   *First voice:*   **How did it happen?**

Second voice: **Prison.**

First voice: **Sad to get in prison**

Happy make in prison

To that happy place

Happy!

♦   *First voice:*   **What happened?**

Second voice: **A sudden reduction.** [Editor: *Loss of position?*]

And you thought EVP was fun? Don't worry – it is!

But how to make sense of it all?

One final EVP sample from the past, it is of poor quality but it still exists,

♦   **Death is a system.**

That, indeed, is how it seems. For all the use of words like The Departed, Passed On, and Transition, there does seem to be a system there, and it would be better not to gloss over it.

OK – as if all this weren't enough, it would seem that there are also false Gods –

♦ **"Worship me"** – said a voice in a recent recording, and possibly false "Heavens" or even "Hells."

It may be – and here we are reminded of the Donovan recordings – that that which one worships in the physical life may become one's Master in the non-physical.

This is also how some writers in the past envisioned Hell, and indeed it might be the same principle that we find in this saying of Jesus.

> *'For it shall be easier for a camel to pass through the eye of a needle than for a rich man to enter the Kingdom of Heaven.'*

He who is nothing passes through with ease – he who won't give up his baggage gets stuck in the entrance.

Just personal spiritual hygiene.

OK – all this is only one aspect of EVP but it is useful stuff to know.

What can we get out of it?

Follow your dream. Blindly following impulses as a way of life may lead to you losing.

If what you say or do – including what you have read here – arouses fury or arouses a general hostility – like having "stirred up a hornet's nest", be quite cool. It is just a phenomenon.

Chapter Seven

God and religions

You wonder where God fits into all this.

Everybody will have his or her own idea about that, and there is no general EVP view about it. But I'll tell you about one very profound utterance that got recorded about the same time as those you read about in the previous part.

But long before that – and long after it – you would get quite a lot of religious stuff.

Early on I tended to be referred to as The Priest (I am neither an Anglican nor a Roman Catholic nor even very religious). The IU was referred to as 'The Box' – thus utterances such as,

♦ **'Here's The Priest with The Box'.**

Although very obviously a woman, Barbara Jennison – the lady who investigated the Chakras – was also referred to as **'The Priest'** on one occasion.

Another time one my employees, Gus, and myself had just returned from lunch to the lab, and switched the equipment on. Immediately it spoke.

♦ **"Hallo Priestesses!"**

Gus, who did not know about EVP, was shocked. (We worked on other things to make the money to be able to fund my EVP research.)

For a time one seemed to access a level where almost every speaker had a title – Doctor or Bishop or Lord.

♦ **'Father Daniel's got the pip',**

was one.

Now I do not know who Father Daniel is/was nor what 'got the pip' means, exactly, it sounds rather an old-fashioned phrase.

♦ **"Doctor Chicago",**

was another. I thought at first that what the voice was saying had to be "Doctor Zhivago" as in the book by Boris Pasternak and the movie of the same name starring Omar Sharif and Julie Christie. But I heard the name again and it was definitely Doctor Chicago – and he was going to give a speech. It sounded as though he was shouting, sounding fierce – though I could not make out any of it – but sounding more like a Chicago gangster than a Doctor of any kind that I knew of. A lot of this stuff sounds pretty "Trekky."

There seemed to be a rule in EVP at that time, and it still holds, that the less the speaker says the clearer and louder it is – and the longer the utterance the less easy it is to understand what is being said.

Another instance of that was when a voice said **'This is Mystic Broadcasting.'**

Well, that went on and on – a low level murmuring, but I was totally unable to make anything of it.

The very first instance of that type of thing in my experience was what the voice called **'The Church of the Seven Stars'** – but beyond the name I can tell you nothing more.

There seems to be a level of excessively vain Informational creatures who are all addressed by titles such as those I have mentioned, who hunt each other down. There is a lot of fear.

Where are the People of the Past?

The fact that we seldom get old-fashioned language, if ever, and all the utterances seem to be in our modern language, is curious.

This is part of the truth about EVP – the facts that are glossed over – not even mentioned.

Where are all the people of the past?

It is not as though there is no language link. We have all read some Shakespeare, some Bible, some Classic books – seen the stories on movies and TV. The language is there.

'Romeo Romeo wherefore art thou Romeo?'

Where is the old-fashioned language?

Its not like the language link -where if one speaks English one tends to get EVP in English – if one doesn't speak Hungarian then one tends not to get any Hungarian EVP.

Its not as though we dont know old-fashioned language, the linkages are there – so why dont we get any? They just don't seem to appear – not for me, nor for anyone, not for any of the many hundreds of honest researchers.

Such a small point, one would think...

But no. No way. Just sit down and have a think about it for a moment....

There is something odd going on here – and everyone is ignoring it.

What about all those people who died 20 years ago – who were born before the World Wars, in Victorian times? What about the people who died even earlier, 30, 40, 50 and more years ago – who were alive at the time of the Wild West, the Boer War, the Crimean War, the Civil War?

What about people who lived through past centuries – many of whom would not speak English as we know it, today?

Where are the people of the past? What is going on? There should be *more* people from the past on the "Other Side" as they call it, than new arrivals.

The other side should be full of people saying, "Gee whillikins, howdy pardner!" "Gadzooks and odds bodkins!" "Art thou well, Brother?" and so on.

It is not as though we don't get accents and dialects and odd expressions in EVP now and then – but where are the people who have gone before? Where are they all?

To be a researcher – not just in EVP, but in most other things – look out for detail – and ask awkward questions. The trouble with EVP is there are not enough people asking awkward questions. That is how radio and TV came into existence originally. The whole idea of wireless communication was crazy – everybody knew that back in 1870. EVP, in its 50 years of existence has grown its own establishment. They will be very upset to hear you doing it – but question everything. You will be expected to listen and applaud – not to ask questions.

Arthur C. Clarke, the science fiction writer (the Movie 2001 for example) and inventor (communication satellites) had this to say about the nature of established opinions and those who promote them.

> 'When a distinguished but elderly scientist states that something is possible, he is almost certainly right. When he states that something is impossible, he is very probably wrong.'[12]

So – can we *dare* to question the established view that Spiritualism has the answers that explain the phenomenon of EVP?

Lets do it. We have had enough "mierde"[13] heaped on us from the AAEVP over the years not to be too alarmed by a few tons more.

How can we explain the lack of old-fashioned voices?

Sarah Estep, ex-schoolteacher founder of the AAEVP, chided me for this attitude in a previous book[14] and pointed out that while on a visit to the pyramids of Egypt, where she felt she was "coming home", she recorded a lot of EVP within one of the Pyramids, in Modern English.[15] And this is the sort of thing that people want to hear. One possible explanation may be in 4 below.

How can we explain the lack of old-fashioned voices? My answer, is simply that, to be honest, we don't yet know,.

But here are some possible answers.

---

[12] Arthur C. Clarke, "Hazards of Prophecy: The Failure of Imagination" (Clarke's First Law) (1962; rev. 1973).

[13] Mierde – (Spanish), Excrement.

[14] 'The Mystery of The Voices.' It was only available on a CDROM.

[15] 'Voices of Eternity', Sarah Estep, being re-issued by Llewellyn Books, 2005.

1. The whole thing has nothing to do with dead people and the Other Side – there are only informational parasites, feeding on memories and hopes, mimicking.

Against that we have the coded messages already mentioned, so the case for this possible answer is undermined by them.

2. The Roman Catholic idea of purgatory may have something going for it. It would explain also why so much of my EVP has involved Irish and Catholics to a disproportionate extent, although I am neither Irish nor Roman Catholic.

Why, for example, should I get this –

♦   **"Bobby Sands Lives!"**

Bobby Sands was an Irish Catholic Hunger Striker who was allowed to die in the brutal days of the 80s.

Professor Wiseman would have you believe that in EVP you hear noises and then you have the illusion of hearing something else – you hear what it is you want to hear. I think not. With respect to Bobby Sands, hearing the above was a total surprise.

I think this option has a lot going for it. It would explain why we only hear those of recent times, and a lot of people exhibiting distress and guilt. The others, presumably, would have moved on. They worked away their guilt, or perhaps got *a good lawyer and a favorable joo-ray*!

3. The people we hear are those who have not yet raised their vibrations to the point where they ascend to a higher energy level and thus lose touch with us.

This is really very similar to 2 but with some pseudo-science added in. It is possible.

4. The means by which the voices are produced is via the "word-library" that we have stored in our brain[16], through which we can recognize the words that we know and can connect with their meanings. This is quite a technical

---

[16] The Phonological Loop.

argument and it would be best read in the paper that I wrote for the Society of psychical Research, published in their March 2004 Journal.

5. Reincarnation keeps sending people forward to their next life after some stabilization period. In other words, the voices that we hear are of those who have not yet reincarnated.

Death may come as a relief to some, especially if they have an undoubted belief in the hereafter, but with the sense of inexorable loss, when all that we have will be taken away, there is bound to be trauma.

Many voices seem to be in distress and among them the word 'victim' is common.

Now I have never seen a ghost, but assuming that they exist, according to the reports of ghosts the ghost is always that of the victim – the lady who had her head chopped off, the child who died in the fire, and so on.

It is not the man with the ax who turns up as a ghost – it is his unfortunate victim, the lady with her head tucked underneath her arm.

And that gives us a rule in an area where there is nothing much but mystery.

So, the general rule is that it is victims that tend to hang around.

One idea of how this might come about. The person seeing a horrifying death approaching will be in such an unimaginable state of mind, with maximum commitment of mental resources, with every last fiber of their being, trying to prevent the inevitable – trying to stop the future happening.

Mentally, they will be trying to stop the future happening.

The result, it is suggested, is a stuck moment in time, a local "stuckness" – which in some way, sensitives can become aware of.

We are really getting away from the subject of EVP here but I just wanted to raise the idea of stuckness as a real thing, and to suggest that in the hereafter there may be some localized stuckness there too.

What the reincarnation idea suggests is that the people of the present were, in the past, the people of the past – it is a case of recycling, and recycling until we get release from the cycle – the Eastern way of putting it. The wheel that you see in the center of the flag of India symbolizes that wheel of life and death.

We tend to think of reincarnation as an Eastern philosophy, but according to St. Thomas it was part of the beliefs of the early Christian church – and, even before that, among the ever practical Celtic peoples, belief in the principle of passing from life to life was so strong and so common, that persons of high family, when considering imminent death would choose another family of good repute into which to be reborn.

Charles Squire, writing in 'Celtic Myths and Legends'[17] says,

> 'The hero Cuchulainn was urged by the men of Ulster to marry, because they knew that his rebirth would be of himself.'

The hero Cuchulainn, incidentally, in legend visited the Isle-of-Skye, here, where a female warrior queen taught him the martial arts.

Another Irish hero was Finn mac Coul, and turning again to 'Celtic Myths and Legends', we read,

> 'Another legend tells how the famous Finn mac Coul was reborn, after two hundred years, as an Ulster king called Mongan.'

And again there is a Skye connection – one of the high hills around the village of Portree is called Finn's Seat (Fingal's Seat.)

Returning now to our question as to what actually happens after a person's body becomes beyond repair, the reincarnation

---

[17] 'Celtic Myths and Legends', Charles Squire, Lomond Books, Parragon, Bath, England.

option is certainly attractive – although I think that elements of all four options might add up to a reasonable theory.

Right now – we don't have the experimental evidence to be able to state – without prejudice – what the truth is. Maybe you can help mankind reach that truth.

The trouble with EVP is that most people came to it with preconceptions and saw in it a way of strengthening their preconceptions.

'Vanity of vanities, all is vanity, saith the Preacher.'

Not many are just looking for the truth.

And how about God – have we learnt anything about God from EVP.

We have certainly learned about "the other fellow". For example,

A woman or child screaming in terror, a deep voice:

♦ **"Meet Satan."**

Evidence so far is that these are dramatizations – there is nothing to fear and the voices are relatively weak and ineffectual and trying to compensate for that by sounding dangerous. Probably, for those without a body and without any clear belief or concept, perhaps mixed up and feeling guilty, such informational beings may prove a threat – a temporary trap. The terms "informational" and "spiritual" can be interchanged. A body gets beyond repair – dies – the spiritual being remains – information is not destroyed.

I do not recall any references to God, except for one, and it took me 15 years to recognize how absolutely profound it was.

There are references to Heaven and Hell – but, in my experience, terms categorizing a being have not been used – terms such as devil or angel have not been found yet.

The word spirit does appear now and then.

Now – about the same time as the phrases I mentioned earlier,

♦ **'Help me. Donovan,'** and so on,

another recording was made. What it said was,

♦   **'God is above Reality.'**

Cool – I thought, a very modern way of sidestepping the issue. God is above reality – so let's not argue about it. Cool.

Fifteen years later, in writing my first book and writing the phrase down, it hit me.

This is certainly the most profound thing ever recorded in EVP – if I had never recorded anything else this one thing was worth it.

Now, all the arguments among the theologians, and among the different religious followers seem less important.

Remember religions are human organizations and as such are imperfect.

In most North European countries now, only a minority believe in God.

The usual way of explaining why is to say, 'Well – I don't believe in the old man in the Sky with a beard, anymore....' This is quite a good way of presenting your position and disarming your listener at the same time.

Your listener has either to accept your position (which is what you want) or to come up with some ridiculous explanation about there really is an old man up there in the sky but we cant see him because blah-blah.

So you get people who believe there is <u>no</u> old man up in the sky, and you get people who believe there <u>is</u> an old man up there in the sky.

So what we have is the familiar situation of two true-believers opposing each other. One believes Yes and the other believes No.

And both are dragging around mental baggage with them – because the situation is unresolved. The non-believer is not actually cool – a free spirit.

They are constantly, (on the back burner – subconsciously if you like), maintaining their belief that there is **no** old guy up there. This is a fixed drain on their mental energy – it affects their behavior, even if only slightly. It affects how they come at people. In the beginning, and especially, if they are young, they will be keen to show that they are not so stupid as to believe in The Old Man In The Sky, by being up-front rude, approving and applauding un-morality – morals being part of The Old man In The Sky deal. And their behavior is used to reinforce that person's position. It reflects their belief, and the behavior reinforces the belief, and the belief reinforces the behavior.

So, you get modified behavior resulting from a modified belief – that's all I am saying – there is no condemnation of anyone – just an explanation of a natural process.

And the same is true of the believer in The Old Man in the Sky – especially if they just switched over to that belief. Their behavior will also be modified. And their behavior will reflect their belief and will reinforce it.

Call it the belief-behavior-belief cycle.

In maintaining a belief, particularly if you live in a society that is in conflict with itself, there is a continual energy loss – even though it is just a faint background stress.

Maintaining a belief is easiest to do if you are mostly involved with others of the same belief and behavior. Thus you tend to get clusters of like-minded people, and if they bond they form "congregations."

But now we read,

♦ **"God is above Reality"**

Reality is, first of all, of course, the physical universe.

This makes sense in a whole lot of ways but the most immediate one and such a huge relief to many is that you don't have to believe in an Old Man with a Beard in the Sky – that is part of reality and God is above reality. You can relax.

Also, if you believe there is no Old Man with a Beard in the Sky – then you too can relax, because God is above Reality. You don't have to keep disbelieving.

Taking the Christian belief as an example, this makes sense in several ways.

But let us start with the common core for Jews, Muslims and Christians – God is the Creator – not the Creation – the Creation is Reality, and includes us while we are in it – we are part of Reality.

Even though a teenager may complain to a parent, 'You are so Unreal...', well no – at that point they are even more real.

And as we know from Moses and the Burning Bush, God just can't appear in Reality. He is the Creator, not the Creation. You dont have to get into Kings and Lords and Masters and all that earthly stuff to explain it. He is the Creator not the Creation.

And that is why He had to have the Prophets and Jesus to be here – in Reality – on his behalf.

The Buddhists have a saying that God has 10,000 faces. In the ancient Chinese numbering system "ten thousand" was the biggest number there was – like "infinity" to us. And this is how they explain why all the different religions see God in different ways – they each see only one face. And this is a nice way of suggesting an end to all the religious squabbling that goes on.

But looking at it from our new perspective – what we would say is, no, it is not God that has 10,000 faces, God is above reality – what you call the faces are just the limited way that limited humans see Him.

So, Allah is the way that Muslims see God, Yahweh is the way that Jews see God, the Holy Trinity is the way that Christians see God.

All this is cool – except when one lot says that *theirs* is the right view and all the others are wrong – in other words, everybody is deceived but us.

From our perspective, don't divide God up just because your vision is narrowed.

OK – enough of the "churchy" stuff – all I am saying is that this is the most profound thing that has come up on EVP so far.

I am not going to go on and on about it and I don't intend to get preachy about it – but (as Lt. Colombo would say) – aah – jus' one more thing, sir, ...

Reality.

Reality – well, yes, first of all that is the physical universe – but to each and everyone of us what is in our minds – the memories, feelings, thoughts, decisions, positions and attitudes that are very personal and very real to us – are also part of reality.

Summing up – the way things seem to be is as follows.

☐ You have God – who is above Reality,

☐ There is another area or areas inhabited by informational (non-physical) beings, some of whom are in distress, and there is talk of being banned or barred or excluded – all of which mean virtually the same thing, and may indicate that "death" is a system of some kind.

This is reinforced by some of the latest results using the AIS V.7 where we are getting voices communicating with each other as though participating in some kind of operation or operations.

☐ There seems to be in a few cases worship of what one might call false gods, which may be a carry forward from the physical universe, with these false gods leading to false heavens.

Although there has been no known harm from any of this, it is still recommended that persons with mental problems should not practice EVP, it is still a research technique and is thus unpredictable.

And it is thoroughly recommended to carry out research in a group – that itself seems to magnify results. The next chapter suggests some ways to carry out a session.

Chapter Eight

a session is like

...ing to get one's feet wet and go and do

...ld days – stop analyzing it – go an... ...that way.

The t... ...d at it – I did try, but it didn't work. ... So – how should one start?

The basic es... ...se,

The Essentials

- A source of White or other Noise, (call that the Source Sound,)

- A recorder of some kind. This is used to record the Source Sound during a Session – in the hope that on playback the sound will contain voices.

For the source of White Noise I recommend our future CD – it also has Pink Noise and Brown Noise on there. These are just different "colors" of White Noise. I have added some Spiricom noise and some "multicolored" 'Tartan' noise.

To begin with that is your source of sound energy. Try one minute of each one and choose the best. Don't run it too loud – there seems to be a maximum sound level where conversions to EVP can occur.

What seems to happen is that the acoustic energy of the Source Sound gets converted to EVP.

The Source Sound should be running at a level just below "easy-to-listen-to" but louder than where you have to strain to pick it up.

Quieter than the TV – at a sort of background music level – except of course what you have is Source Sound rather than music.

Dont worry about hitting it at just the right level first time – in truth there is no single right level – what you are getting here are just the rules to give you the best chance of scoring right away. If you don't – don't worry – remember it took me two years of trying to succeed – and then I needed Alpha Technology to do so.

With time you may discover and use your own rules – for your own situation and your own room.

The Experimental Laboratory

You should choose a quiet room to do your EVP in. Try to stick to the same place all the time. It should be free from sounds such as dogs barking, birds whistling, neighbors shouting, cars revving up, toilets flushing and so.

Ensure that where you sit the chair does not move or make creaking, cracking or scraping sounds. Ensure that anyone else allowed in is told to stay silent.

Avoid sneezes, gasps, coughs – just ensure that your room is as silent as possible. Doing this is for your own benefit. If when you come to playback there is a sound that might be a door slamming, or it might be someone saying 'Aha!' – then analyzing this could be a lengthy procedure.

There are no special times to do it – but a well-known investigator has always used 10 in the morning. This is quite a good time anyway. The rush hour is over, the kids have gone to school, people have gone to work, and the cat is sleeping off last night's adventures....

The recorder microphone – or the machine itself, if it uses a built-in mic – should be placed two to three feet – about 70 to 100 cms – from the speakers that the sound is coming from. A built-in mic is not ideal as it is apt to pick-up motor noise.

Traditionally, what were used were open-reel tape recorders.

Later, cassette recorders became common and most of my own work has been done on cassette.

An improvement can be found as far as EVP is concerned with the modern small hand held speech recorders.

These contain special speech circuits – psycho-acoustic circuits – which boost the response to speech sounds enormously.

They are available in both analog (tape) and digital (solid-state) form.

If in doubt consult the manufacturers or distributors – do not latch on to rumors rushing around the EVP world for truth – regrettably there is usually some personal reason for someone trashing one kind of recorder or another – sometimes the "technical explanations" you get amount to outright superstition!

'Caveat Emptor' (let the buyer beware) as they used to say in Ancient Rome!

Just be sensible – ask the manufacturer. Meanwhile – my recommendation is to use any hand-held speech recorder – analog or digital – with a slight edge going to the digital because of its naturally noise-free background.

When doing an EVP session it is not recommended that you actually hold the machine in your hand, rest it on a stable surface at the recommended distance from the loudspeaker.

List of Commonly Used Recorders.

Here are some hand-helds that are in common use,

- Radio Shack CTR-122 (this also has a speed adjustment that can be useful in advanced editing)

- Sanyo M-110C

- Olympus 5711, 5712, and 5713 micro-cassette recorders

- Panasonic RR-DR60 (Digital)

And some larger, quality, decks,

- AIWA HXPRO Stereo Cassette Deck AD-R470

- MEMOREX SCT-87 High Speed Dubbing Stereo Cassette Deck

Or you could use a PC or laptop with a sound card, but the advantage of the psycho-acoustic circuits in the modern hand-helds will be lost. Windows has its own virtual recorder – but you would be better getting one of the specialized software audio editing systems instead.

- Acoustica

- Cool2000

- Cool Pro

- Gold Wave

- Sonic Foundry

Among EVP people the most popular one is Cool – and this is available in two forms Cool2000 and Cool Pro. Cool2000 has more than adequate functionality for EVP Research – in fact a lot of it is not needed. I am informed that Adobe has now taken over Cool and no longer supply Cool 2000.

Cool Pro is ideal for those who want "top-of-the-range" but it intended for music makers and is a massive over-kill and waste of money for EVP work. It is capable of acting as a 64 track-deck – ideal for music producers – but for speech – don't be silly! Again it has several scientific filter functions – and you really need to be a highly qualified specialist in that area to know what you are doing.

If someone is Bs'ing you about it – ask them, 'Should I use a Butterworth or a Tschebyshev filter for EVP, and why?'

In actual fact, for voice work it doesn't matter at all. Pro is fine for music producers, 2000 is a better match for EVP.

The Psycho-Acoustic circuit is probably the biggest advance in EVP work since results were boosted by sound-editing software becoming available.

Session Scripts

Here are rules that may help with the actual EVP session.

1. Write down a script of what you want to say. Allow around 8 seconds of silence between each sentence.

2. Switch on the recording; wait 3 seconds in silence and then say START.

3. Then proceed with your script, remembering the silences.

4. When the script is complete, say End of Session and switch off the recording.

You should try to make a session fairly short as analyzing what you have got is going to take time – perhaps 30 minutes analyzing for a 3-minute session. The time will come when you won't need that long as you will be able to reject most of what you hear as not coming up to your highest standards. But don't reject anything at the beginning – you never know what you might miss.

Noise Reduction

If you have noise reduction software then here is what to do. Display the session on the sound editor. Highlight the bit of the display between switch-on and you saying START. Use this in the sound-editor to get the Noise Reduction profile.

If you need more information or want a sound-editor then we are planning to arrange with a well-known maker of sound-editors to have one available to you to download, with its own special manual for use with EVP.

You can find out about this by contacting **Skyelab.co.uk** online.

Whether you use a Sound Editor or not here is what to listen for.

EVP comes in many different forms.

1. **Normal speech** – and this has three forms,

    1.1. **Normal** for a man,

    1.2. **Normal** for a woman,

    1.3. **Normal** for a child.

2. **Whisper speech.**

3. **Hoarse whisper speech.**

4. **Robotic speech.** Sometimes this can sound like someone speaking with an artificial larynx.

5. **Squawk speech** – like that of a parrot.

6. **Chirp speech** – like that of a budgerigar.

7. **Whistle speech** – a bird-like sound.

8. **Choral speech** – where two or more voices are speaking at the same time, saying the same thing. (Not to be confused with two people speaking at roughly the same time – interrupting each other, for example).

9. **Morphs** – this where a voice gets transformed into something else. Listen to your own voice during the playback. Is that what you actually said? Is it in the script? This is why we use scripts – so that we have in writing the only things that were said during a session.

   So, for example, if what you said according to the script was, **'I will repeat that,'** and on replay a voice said, instead,

   'Its a lifeline.'

   then morphing – one sound changing into another – has occurred. One has to be careful with morphing – you can get some of the best voices through morphing – just test your hearing by having someone else listen to it too.

   Nothing destroys the credibility of EVP more than people rushing out to publicize utterances no one else can hear!

   This – and the smell of cats - is what ended the BBCs involvement with EVP.

10. ERVs (Event Related Voices.)

These can be similar to Morphs, but can also be different. If some one coughs, or there is the sound of a passing car or if a door is slammed somewhere, in terms of sounds, these are what we call Events. Now, sometimes, not very often, you will find that just after the event is a voice. It may be so close in time to the Event that the utterance actually begins during the utterance. Like Morphs – you have to exercise care over what you hear. If you are smart with a sound editor you should copy the ERV by itself and paste it into a separate file – leaving the Event itself behind in the session record – that way you can listen to the ERV in isolation. This and other techniques are part of the EVP Master Class run at Portree and elsewhere.

11. Thread related.

Finally, this is a new category of utterances, where one utterance is a comment on or response to an utterance that went before. They are related by a contextual thread. The longest thread we have had so far is about nine utterances.

EVP at its present stage is not like a telephone – the fault may not be with the equipment or the experimenter – the fault may lie with the *listener* – who is also part of the system. There are a number of things that are barriers to understanding EVP.

A. Hearing Problems

It is well known that hearing decays with age – and by age I don't mean old – I mean over 25, in some cases. And even then there is no guarantee that the hearing is good. It is well known from scientific research into hearing, that prolonged listening to loud music, or being a drummer, or working in a noisy environment without ear defenders, can damage hearing.

If you want to check your hearing using a test called the monosyllabic word test – a version of which is used by the US military – there is a self-score listening test at www.skyelab.co.uk. If you score more than 10 or more correct, your hearing is fine. If you score less than 10 correct then you might consider having tests done – just to check up on what is happening.

It may be OK, perhaps you are not yet an 'Expert Listener', but it may be you could do with having your hearing attended to. Makers of hearing accessories like Siemens advertise free hearing tests at their hearing consultant distributors for the over 60s. It should be possible to find a consultant who will do tests at a very reasonable rate, whatever your age.

Hearing deficiencies that go un-noticed in ordinary life may still interfere with interpreting EVP. And people tend to be a bit vain about their hearing. 'Don't be ridiculous!' they will say, 'There's nothing wrong with my hearing – my father had perfect hearing well into his nineties!'

Sometimes just an ear syringing by your local nurse to remove excess natural earwax is all that is needed.

So that is one barrier – hearing problems. The next one is not so easy.

B. Listening Problems

Accents

Listening problems can start with being used to hearing only one dialect of English all the time – not having any exposure to any other forms.

Most English speakers tend to think that the way that they speak English is the standard way – they can't hear any accent.

'Oh – I just love your English accent' an American may say, and the English person will just smile politely, thinking, 'I dont have an accent – its Americans who speak with an accent.'

Fortunately this is not a problem – especially when the conversation goes on for a while and you can also lip-read – which we all do, subconsciously.

But when you get just a quick – less than two seconds – bunch of words bursting out of the blue at you that is another matter.

Whoosh – there and gone.

Almost all normal voiced speech is in what seems to be the person's home accent and that can be quite difficult to most people to understand. Let's just look at a few examples of this.

'God bless coop of lie.' (Actually, **'God bless cup of lye.'**)

'Joojmin!' (Actually, **'Judgment!'**)

Finally, this one would probably be quite incomprehensible to anyone not familiar with the accent of the North East of Scotland. Imagine playing this to someone in Montgomery, Alabama – they would be convinced that (a) you were crazy, or (b) That EVP was an illusion – or both!

They would also tell you they didn't have any kind of accent at all, leastwise, not so's you-all 'd notice....

You will actually find more Elizabethan English in the Southern and Eastern States than in all of EVP. These are the people who speak the real Queen's English. So here is one of the many Scottish dialects.

First voice: **"Ey mither.'** ('Hey Mother!')

Second voice: **'Oos'ere?** (Who is there?)

First voice: **"Sno arthir.'** (It is not Arthur)

Third voice: **'Suzannah Vega!'** (Googling on the off chance that there might be a 'Suzannah Vega' there I found that Suzanne Vega is quite a well-known singer.)

And then, occasionally there are words that dont seem to match up with anything,

'Help me Dr. Greystone, help me up, I'm lying on a benster.' What is a 'benster?' I still have not found a meaning for it.

First voice: **'Very cold....'** (Possibly an Indian accent)

Second voice: **'Where is....'** (Last portion cannot be made out.)

Third voice: **Savant 'is lungs...'** (Pronounced **'loongs'**.)

What is 'Savant' – some sort of medical term? It is pronounced as 'Sa-<u>vant</u>' not as the French word, 'Savant.'

So – does anyone know what a 'benster' is, or what 'to sa<u>vant</u>' means?

Language Problems

As has already been mentioned, EVP tends to be in the language of the experimenter.

'Tends' is a word that we engineers like to use – it is like a get-out clause, what it says is that though this is what normally happens, it is possible – even if rarely – that something else may happen instead.

What I am indicating here is that – very rarely – you may get a word in a language you may not understand.

To illustrate how rare an event this is – in hundreds of hours of experiments over years and years I only got two words I did not understand.

The first one I should have known about, living on the Isle-of-Skye as I do.

The words were, **'An Cladach.'** I was fairly sure this was Gaelic, as the word 'an' means 'the' in English and the other word with its 'ach' ending sounded right, too.

But I had to look it up.

What it means in English is 'The Shore'. And, as you may know, 'The Shore' is quite common terminology with Christians referring to going to Heaven.

The second case was much less reputable.

It went as follows,

'Viva – vive Les Grotins'

Well, I had done French at school so I knew what 'Vive' meant, and since learning some Italian and Spanish I now know what Viva means – it means the same thing, "Long live!" But it looks as though the voice was getting a bit confused with languages – beginning first with 'Viva' and immediately correcting it to 'Vive.'

The next bit I thought I knew, 'Croutons' – these are the little bits of bread you put in your soup. But it sounded as though the person was mis-pronouncing it as 'Grotins.' Was this a dialect? I sent a copy of it to my friend in Paris, David Mackenzie Thornton, who was a frequent Alpha Technology user. Shortly afterwards I got a phone call from David. 'It is a legitimate word, Alec,' he advised me, 'But I wouldn't put them in your soup – it means horse-shit!'

We fell about laughing both ends of the line.

Yes, the saying, 'Viva, Vive Les Grotins' (long live the horseshit) was in fact typical of the less than reverend way some regarded EVP.

In fact I would say that there is a selection of the voices that seem to be uppity, opinionated and willing to have a laugh at anything.

So – getting the occasional foreign word is something to be aware of – though, so far, it seems to happen very rarely.

Background Noise

No matter how good an utterance is, if the background noise level is too high, then it cannot be properly understood. We call this problem the Signal to Noise Ratio (SNR) where the 'signal' means the voice you are wanting to here.

Background noise can from all sorts of sources,

-       Appliances inside and outside the house,

-       Television and radio,

- Passing traffic,

- Neighbors,

- Slamming doors, creaking chairs, and other noises normal in an occupied house,

- Using cassette tape to record, or other above average noisy methods of recording.

- Using a high impedance microphone such as a crystal Mic,

- Using old-fashioned amplifiers of the tube (valve) type.

To get best results you should avoid all of the above where applicable. It may not seem that doing this is going to get you any more voices, but it will – because almost certainly there are voices there, buried in noise, that would normally get overlooked. You'd be surprised at how tiny some utterances are.

And after you have taken care of that, there is an even more important way to avoid bad SNR, and that is to ensure that when you listen to the playback you do so in quiet surroundings. Good headphones are not expensive and are probably the best way to listen to a playback when doing analysis – that is – searching for voices.

My recommendation is *never* to allow EVP recordings to be used as proof of EVP by playing samples to a hall-full of people – or even to a small group.

The reasons for this are,

- You can't control the SNR.

- You dont know what states their hearing is in.

- No on is listening on headphones, the room acoustics may be wrong, you may get echoes and dead spots.

- They could well be approaching the whole thing with suspicion – as a group attitude – in which case you are the odd one out – and you become the target. Basic group psychology. Nothing evil about it – we dont have to invent enemies or conspiracies to explain what happens.

I do not know of anyone – anyone – who went around convincing people of the credibility of EVP by playing samples – on the contrary I have seen some pretty smart people "fold up and die" – trying to do this.

- The listeners' expectations of EVP may be so high than even your best efforts will be a great disappointment.

- You do not know how good or bad they are at understanding other people's accents, and poor speech – with few exceptions none of the voices I have heard have shown any signs of being trained speakers!

Notes:

i. EVP research belongs in research not in public display.

ii. Skyelab 1 has a free introductory course at our Portree facility, for those who want to view the results – where everyone gets a hearing test – but do the online test, first, and everyone listens on headphones. Places are limited so make an advance reservation please. As the course is free – travel and housing assistance is not available – the website EVPSITE has links to Skye Tourist and other sites.

Groups

One of the things we recommend is the setting up of groups – some of the best results were obtained in a group setting.

With Archie MacDonald, Mike Scott, the Financial Director and his engineer and myself we had 5 present at that (the Margaret/Molly) session.

At the Palace Hotel session (Lezzillee. This is it. David) we had over 20 present.

Here is some guidance to provide you with the best chances.

Set out in advance what your objectives are – if you meet weekly, try to set your objectives on a monthly basis. Don't be afraid to change your plans if your results warrant that.

The Monaghan Experiment

The other thing that happens to help analysis is being able to see the utterance on your PC – so you can hear and see at the same time. Often a little blip on the screen can help you locate where a voice is, buried in noise.

During the making of the documentary by DMP for Channel 4 in the UK the producer, David Monaghan asked me to take an Alpha to just beside a roaring waterfall. Of course the recording that resulted was just wall-to-wall noise. But by listening very closely, and watching the screen intently, to my great surprise voices were found. The sound was then cleaned up using the sound editor to produce a fairly noise free result. The voices were not very good – but it was amazing that there were any voices there at all.

Both at the waterfall and at the laboratory in California the voices that were recorded were very poor. From experience I can say that the system does not like being relocated.

The same may not be true for the hand-held recorders, however – in fact one, the Sanyo, gave spectacular results when taken to the scene of a number of road crashes – also the area where in the past several people reported seeing 'the ghost car' of Skye.

Unfortunately, I have never seen a ghost or a UFO – so if an old cynic like me tells you how wonderful EVP is then there must be something to it.

And there is.

Chapter Nine

EVP Aids

Voices in EVP experiments are not very frequent nor very clear – without some sort of aid.

When I first heard about EVP and began experimenting, there were only three people in the UK who were into EVP.

There was Gilbert George (GG) Bonner, a Canadian trained in hypnotherapy, who lived in St. Leonard's, a seaside town in Sussex. Gilbert was the first person in the UK to get into EVP and he had a real talent for research. One of his samples of an EVP voice is probably still the best voice ever in EVP. It is a lady's voice, very clear, almost bell-like, very Other-Side, and she says,

♦ **'Doesn't Bonner look ridiculous!'**

It was a Friday night, and Gilbert, a sane and sensible guy in case anyone should think otherwise, had had a glass or two of red wine – falling asleep on his couch as the recording went on. It went on for at least an hour – you had to wait a long time for voices in those days – apart from that GG was asleep on his couch anyway.

Imagine his surprise and amusement when on replay he heard this female saying in her angelic voice, **'Doesn't Bonner look ridiculous!'**

GG died a few years ago – he had amassed thousands of recordings and it was his complaint – as it is with the rest of us, that there seemed to be absolutely no support for EVP research. Not only was there no funding but one was constantly having to fend off those who thought you were competing with them and who wanted to elbow their way to the front.

Around the same time as GG pioneered EVP in the UK so too did Raymond Cass – a hearing specialist who also got good results. However, he had left EVP by the time I found out about it, leaving only the three Die-hards. But, even now, when new people want to find 'The Expert' on EVP they go to find Raymond Cass (now deceased). Just as when they want to find out the best system they go to find out about the "Spiricom" – which we will discuss later.

At that time the Three Die-hards exchanged cassette tapes – discussing theories and sending each other the latest samples of our work – except that I hadn't got any samples to send!

The next member of the group was Richard Sheargold – quite a well-known authority on EVP who was a member of the Society for Psychical Research (SPR).

The SPR was founded in the 19th Century by a group of Scientists at Cambridge to investigate psychic phenomena using the disciplines of scientific research.

Three founders of the SPR: Frederick Myers, Edmund Gurney, & Henry Sedgwick.

Sheargold had written a booklet on the subject of EVP voices and the SPR had produced a cassette of some of the voices obtained by him.

The third member of the group was Peter Jones B.Sc. who worked on telecommunications research for a government department. During WW 2 he had worked a secret defense establishment with a guy who would later be my first boss when I joined the R&D people at EMI, and later still become famous as Sir Godfrey Hounsfield Nobel Laureate.

I dont know if he ever mentioned EVP to 'H' as Hounsfield was known, but our own little group of EVP people in the UK used to get into some highly technical discussions about what EVP was and how it came about. It is rather sad to hear these same notions still being suggested by people today, as though they were new – 20 years and more on. For all the so-called histories of EVP none of these valuable findings have been mentioned, and in fact some discoveries have been reported as having been made by the writers of the histories! But such is the nature of journalism.

Sheargold used a method he called side-band splash, which I will describe to you presently, while Peter Jones used mostly White Noise.

They would do something like a couple of hours in the evening once or twice a week and get maybe a couple of reasonable voices out of that.

As I had the good fortune of having spent many hours listening to very faint voice sounds in a lot of White Noise when I was engaged on R&D contracts for NASA, (MOL, Skylab, etc.); USN (Sealab2); and others; I was able to pick-up EVP voices very easily, right from the beginning – when listening to other people's examples of course.

So here are the first two methods and the EVP aids that they used.

White Noise (Peter Jones B.Sc.)

Jones had a very straightforward 'rig'. He had a speaker driven by an amplifier driven by a White Noise source, and at some distance he had the recorder – normally a good quality cassette recorder. He varied the source of the White Noise and like me had tried to develop a noise cancellation system – so that all you would be left with then would be the voice sounds.

The way we looked at it then – and it is still substantially true – was that the sound energy in the Source Sound was somehow transformed in whole or in part into sound energy in the form of voice sounds. It was a transformation process.

We knew then, from experience, as I pointed out earlier, that making the Source Sound louder isn't going to make the voices louder – so there was more to it than just a simple transformation process.

There are more technical ways of looking at it, but they are more suited to scientific papers than in a book for the non-scientist.

Like the rest of us, Bonner would try anything to get improved results so he wasn't just restricted to White Noise. To my delight, one of the best results was with a form of noise I called Porridge (which is what we call Oatmeal Mush) based on Bonner's Noise Mixture – which we come to next.

On the CD we plan to have a track that contains a whole session full of continuous White-Noise (3 minutes). There are other variations of White Noise which are used scientifically and these are called Pink Noise and Brown Noise – one sounds a bit more hissy, another a softer hiss and the final one a bit more rumbly.

On the CD also we plan to include a track of Pink Noise (3 minutes) and a Track of Brown Noise (3 minutes).

So, you can try all three of them – an opportunity that Peter never had.

There is also 3 minutes of "Porridge".

Multi-voicing (Bonner)

As I have mentioned we were willing to try anything to get better results – except perhaps for Sheargold, who, was sure he was right and stuck to Sideband Splash – more popularly known as "Mush" – which is where the name for my Scottish noise mixture – Porridge (oatmeal mush) – came from.

One of the things that Bonner had done was this. He had three recorders playing simultaneously as the noise source – and to ensure that there was no English they all played tapes in French – each one different – so there was quite a din – babble in fact. He then recorded all this on a fourth recorder – which we will call the session record.

These methods took a long time of course, and a lot of listening, but you develop an ear for EVP – initially it sends a cold thrill through you – hairs on your neck may stand on end – but soon, you just pick it up because it has that "EVP" sound.

Porridge

The way I looked at it – if the energy of White Noise which is by definition a totally random sound sequence was transformed wholly or partly into EVP plus reduced noise – would it not be a lot more efficient to use as a source sound something which was not random but which included the actual basic sounds of speech – although not in the sounds of words.

Doing it with French tapes was fine – but remember that many of the sounds in the French language do not occur in English and they are already formed into words which means that some sounds have to be discarded as being in the wrong place at the required time.

My approach to producing a new improved sound mixture, Porridge, was to produce a blend of sounds which included all the individual sounds in English – these sounds are called Phonemes – more usually referred to as vowels and consonants.

We already knew that an utterance would only last at the most for two seconds, so the "recipe" for making Porridge is as follows.

You say 'a' for two seconds and record that. You play back the two seconds of 'a' while saying 'e' for two seconds – and the result of that on playback is you saying 'a' and saying 'e' simultaneously for two seconds. You repeat that for all the Phonemes and you end up with a mixture that contains the sounds of all the phonemes in English to use as a Source Sound.

The CD will have a full session's length of Porridge on it.

I also produced a version I called Digital Porridge that was intended to enable noise-cancellation of the type that Peter Jones and I wanted to do. But recording using tape was not an exact enough process to enable that at the time we were doing it, 20 years ago.

Babble

In the last 10 years, Sonia Rinaldi of the Brazil group has invented a method she calls Babble – I dont know if she ever heard of Bonner's work – there is no reason why she should – innovations in any field seldom are made entirely uniquely.

Mush/Sideband Splash (Richard Sheargold)

Sheargold, who was a radio ham and worked as an electronic technician for an aircraft parts company on the outskirts of London, preferred to use a radio method – in spite of the well-known hazards of using a radio – picking up broadcasts or other radio hams.

Nevertheless, if carried out by someone who was used to taking great care and who knew exactly what he was doing, on the basis of long experience – then any objections to this method would have to be theoretical.

So careful was Sheargold that compared with Bonner he did not produce many samples. Either they were not there or were discarded. And of those he circulated to us I found nothing wrong or suspicious.

The way you did this method – and it was similar to the one favored by the early experimenter, Raudive – was you tuned your radio exactly in-between two adjacent am stations.

When you did this you would be liable to hear an occasional spitting – splashing sound – and this was the Sound Source for his EVP experiments.

Although I was not getting any results myself – I had given up trying – some suggested that you had to be a spiritualist medium to get results, my analysis of the results sent on to me indicated that this was a phenomenon – and there was no natural explanation for it.

Spiricom

Then about March 1982 word came out that a researcher in the USA, George Meek, and his technician William O'Neill had made a tremendous breakthrough – not only could they get voices but they could talk to the voices – two-way communication!

As my father had died just three months before, this sounded like the sort of thing I could be interested in.

I wanted to know more and sent off for details. I got a set of leaflets offering the 'Spiricom' at $10, 000. It was a fairly complex unit – but in spite of that I could not see where the price was coming from.

And then, after more study, I could see that there was no way that this equipment would produce the results claimed. I wrote an article on the subject for a group called the ASSAP – the Association for the Scientific Study of Anomalous Phenomena – a sort of breakaway group from the SPR. They published a journal called Common Ground.

The material was also taken up in a book called 'The Afterlife' by Jenny Randles and Peter Hough.[18] After introducing the subject of Spiricom, the authors continue,

> 'It is, however, worth presenting the comments of Alex MacRae. As an EVP researcher himself, he traveled from his home in Scotland to the USA to see Meek. MacRae reported in the objective journal Common Ground that he was impressed by the team's efforts but not altogether convinced by their results.
>
> He cited a contact via Spiricom who appeared to drop in on the link with Dr. Mueller. This was a man who gave his name as Fred Ingstrom and said he had died in rural Virginia in 1830. Firstly, it is slightly curious that if time and space mean nothing in the afterlife all the contacts reported

---

[18] 'The Afterlife', Randles and Hough, Judy Piatkus Publishers, London 1993.

via Spiricom in the USA should be from deceased Americans. Why nobody from other lands?'

Then they continued,

> 'However, MacRae noted from a linguistics point of view that some of the comments by the deceased Fred Ingstrom were a little puzzling. For example he was told 'You sound like a robot' and fully understood the meaning of that expression, even although the word robot was not invented until [*nearly*] a hundred years after his death.'

And finally,

> 'More intriguing is that, as MacRae notes, Fred used terms like 'OK' and 'Oh boy', which would hardly be habitual language in a rural community 160 years ago.'

There is one last statement they quote – which I would probably not make today. One often learns the hard way.

> '... Alex MacRae does admit that the equipment designed for Spiricom is very interesting and offers no reason to suspect the integrity of the people behind it.'

But it was not the above comments (that didn't appear until 1993) that caused such consternation – it was my fairly technical article in Common Ground in 1982.

The Second Story

I hadn't meant to cause such a stir but effectively it pushed Meek into going back to O'Neill to query his explanation, to find out what was *really* going on.

To be quite honest, I wasn't all that impressed by their organization. This was an experience that was to be repeated some twenty years later, with the ION Foundation. Here was one guy (Meek) apparently spending vast sums of money, with a staff of just one technician – and yet he was getting a false story about what was being done. What was going on?

Finally, Meek sent me a copy of the system as it really was — and this time it made sense. The heart of it was a little radio bug of the sort available from electronic hobbyists' shops for a couple of dollars.

The $10,000 price asked for earlier was presumably to help pay off the R&D costs — a not insignificant factor that almost everybody who has not been involved in innovation is unaware of. My own with EVP involvement has cost me more than Meek, so I understand how he felt about it — except that there are a couple of odd points. It is said that Meek used $500, 000 of his own money to fund the Spiricom research.

It is said that he had been around the world four times seeking the wisdom that ended up as the Spiricom.

What a task. But I found no evidence of this wisdom in our long discussions. He gave me a copy of a "Gospel" written by a guy in Kentucky, which told the story of how Jesus had married, and so on. OK — no problem.

He gave me a copy of a paperback called 'The Cosmic Book'. It had been written by a guy who later died in the Chicago air-crash, an event Meek believed was staged to take this guy out, because he knew too much. It has rather a good experiment in the book on how to stop time.

But the real influence on George's thinking was a slim hardback book.

He showed me a book by a NYC "guru" of the 1920s. It seemed typical of the time, reasonably enlightened — quite good in fact. And it was in following these teachings that he had formed the Metascience Foundation, the organization behind Spiricom.

Four Times Around The World

So, perhaps the four journeys around the world had been for another purpose. And four journeys? *Four?*

Was there a problem about learning all this wisdom?

Nevertheless, the four world trips, presumably, was where a lot of the $500,000 had gone.

It certainly didn't go to O'Neill, his sole technician.   J.G.
Fuller, writing about O'Neill's reluctance to go to the
Washington Press Club presentation[19], describes how George
"lent" on O'Neill to persuade him to go,

> 'Meek told him that his future work with the Spiricom
> project was so critical that he had earned an increase in
> his monthly fees that would be enough to cover
> payments on another second-hand car, which was
> essential that he get.'

> 'O'Neill's car had recently broken down and was
> beyond repair.'

A raise large enough to enable payments to be kept up on a
second-hand car – something of a contrast to $500,000.

The Curious Case of the Half Million Dollars

And there is another curious thing about the half a million
dollars. According to J.G. Fuller,

> 'Meek told us that his equipment required major
> funding. "I was lucky enough to get Jim McDonnell,
> chairman of the board of McDonnell-Douglas
> [Aircraft Company], interested in the project," Meek
> said. Jim had been interested in psychic research for a
> long time. ... I worked out a deal with him where he
> would let me go ahead and design and build the
> equipment. He would pay for it, and then lease it back
> to me for a dollar a year. It was a lucky break.'[20]

The question remains – was *this* the reputed $500, 000 of 'his
own money' that Meek poured into the Spiricom?

Turning once again to J.G. Fuller's book, at the Washington
Press Club, after his presentation Meek has this to say,[21]

---

[19] Page 139, 'The Ghost of 29 Megacycles', J.G. Fuller, Signet, 1981.

[20] Page 17, 'The Ghost of 29 Megacycles', J.G. Fuller, Signet, 1981.

[21] Page 153, 'The Ghost of 29 Megacycles', J.G. Fuller, Signet, 1981.

"That is the legacy I want to leave my children and grandchildren." Then he smiled and said to the audience, "And yours. That is why my wife and I have put hundreds and thousands of dollars into this – money we could otherwise leave to our offspring."

That is commendable – but 'hundreds and thousands' do not add up to half a million, and some of that money was his wife's.

Back in April of 1982 Meek sent me a tape of the Spiricom Noise to use as a Sound Source. Unfortunately, no voices have been obtained using this method, but there is a session full (3 minutes) of that Spiricom Source Sound on the CD – maybe you will have better luck.

In actual fact neither Meek himself nor William O'Neill were able to get any more voices after December 1981 – some months before the big publicity occurred. Unfortunately (?) this meant that the device could never be observed in action.

Oh dear.

The Writer and His Art

According to 'The Afterlife', the book quoted above,

'John Fuller, renowned for his high standard of investigation of other paranormal mysteries, became embroiled in the controversy. Ultimately he wrote a book called *The Ghost of 29 Megacycles*. Right from the first page it is obvious that Fuller is uncomfortable with his material.'

Well, as one of those who supplied Fuller with a lot of his material, I did not find him in the least bit "uncomfortable" with his material. On the contrary, it was slightly embarrassing to be addressed in a "conspiratorial" kind of way as, "Someone who can help us make the case for EVP more convincing for the reader."

And then we find that to ensure that he is not being hoaxed,

'... Fuller traveled to England to meet EVP expert Raymond Cass.

I've gone over the tapes time and time again, as an audiophonic expert' he quotes Cass as saying.

Unfortunately there is no such thing as an "audiophonics" expert – Raymond Cass ran a shop selling hearing-aids and so would probably have carried out tests of hearing – sometimes called audiology Perhaps that is what he meant by "audiophonics." And certainly, if your object is to lead your readers on, then "audiophonics expert" is *much* more impressive.

But the question remains – why did Fuller not go to the Dept. of Phonetics at University College London – who are truly world-class experts in speech and hearing – only a taxi ride from the very expensive hotel where he stayed in London?

Or why not go to MIT – who also had a brilliant lab there – and who were located "next door" to his home in Connecticut.

Why travel 6000 miles to visit a hearing aid salesman, and another pretty good self-promoter? Because he could be counted upon to say the right thing – with the added kudos of being an "audiophonics expert" in a foreign country?

They are all dead now, Fuller, Meek, O'Neill – but not one word has been heard from any of them through EVP. Evolution continues.

Meet Meek in an Altered State

But back to spring 1982 – I was so pleased with the new description of the Spiricom that I decided to go and visit George Meek in Franklin, North Carolina, to witness the device in operation. I flew from London Heathrow to Atlanta airport and stayed at a motel at the Airport while waiting to get the OK from the Meeks to come to visit to see the Spiricom.

To keep the story short – I never did get to see it. I kept getting told reasons why I couldn't come. I left Atlanta, spent a week at the Airport Ramada in Nashville, Tennessee, then on to spend a week with my friends the Feolas in Lexington Kentucky where Dr. Feola was doing cancer research at the University there. Eventually I returned via the World Fair at Knoxville to Atlanta and finally met Mr. Meek at Atlanta airport, back in Georgia – he was returning from Florida. We had a long chat – mostly about a new arthritis cure O'Neill had been told how to make by one of their EVP contacts, the late Doctor Mueller, or Doc. It sounded to me like standard radiotherapy – as was common at that time

In fact it was all a bit odd – and some of the excuses as to why I shouldn't come to Franklin NC, where they lived, were really not very credible. Individually the excuses each had some credibility – but when you looked at the whole sequence of them they didn't add up.

Neither did the reason for the Spiricom having stopped working seem credible.

Through Channeling they were told by Doc Mueller that he had gone onto a higher plane – being now more advanced – and so the Spiricom was too gross a method for him to use now.

You'd think that if he was aware of this possibility, and he was as responsible a person as he was represented as being, that he would have said something beforehand on the Spiricom. OK – its a small point, but it makes you wonder.

What was even more strange, however, was the fact that none of the other people who had come through on the Spiricom ever spoke again either. There was no mention of them having moved up a plane as had happened with "Doc", but they too failed to speak again. There was Fred for example – who at one time had quite a lot to say – but somehow the Spiricom didn't seem to work again for him either. And Doc Nick had vanished too.

Saying that the Spiricom had ceased working because Doc had gone up to such a high vibratory rate that he could no longer communicate with us anymore may have sounded good at the time – but accepting that as an excuse left a big hole in the overall logic. What happened to the others?

The channeling may well have happened, but if so they failed to think the logic of the situation through.

What happened to the other two guys who had also been contacted by the Spiricom?

And Doc himself didn't add up too well – at one time he is giving advice to the electronics technician O'Neill about making adjustments to the Spiricom -'You have to match the input transistor -' and he goes on to suggest two component values. This sounds to anyone not into electronics as really impressive hi-tech talk. Actually it is PR and BS – virtually meaningless – and unnecessary. So, although Doc was supposed to be an electronics expert who worked on the space program – it is evident from this piece of hi-tech advice that he didn't know very much about electronics. Yet this is boasted about as one of the proofs of EVP.

Herr Doktor Mueller

Now there was a real Doc Mueller and he worked on the ground test equipment for Missile Tests over the Florida Range – the missiles being roughly the equivalent of Saddam Hussein's 'Scud' missiles today. In actual fact I also worked on ATE (Automatic Test Equipment) for aerospace, at General Dynamics in Rochester NY – but I never heard of this famous engineer, Dr. Mueller – whose qualifications, it seemed to O'Neill,

> '... [exceeded those of] "DR Einstein".[22]

It so happens that there was also another Dr. Mueller who worked on the actual *Space* Program (not Intermediate Range Ballistic Missile tests) at the Cape, and who made a tremendous contribution to it. He is also still alive and active.

There are some that have got the two confused in their minds, and once again I think the source was a German mistranslation by someone trying to boost the image of EVP. But you cannot construct truth from lies – and I should not have to spend half of a book about EVP correcting delusions and

---

[22] Page 90, 'The Ghost of 29 Mega-cycles', Fuller, Signet, 1981.

---

misrepresentations. Anyone would think this is what I do for fun. It is a disgrace.

And so "Doc Mueller the famous space engineer and electronics expert" who moved to a "higher plane" and the "amazing Spiricom" are still big items for newcomers to EVP. Over and over again I have supplied the Spiricom noise to inquirers – after a few months they forget about it. No results. It doesn't work. EVP doesn't work. Point proven.

The biggest conveyor of misinformation regarding Spiricom and Mueller on the web is Keeleynet – avoid it!

I Meet the Meeks on Skye

But going back to 1983 – in April 1983 George Meek and his wife came to the Isle-of-Skye to see me and stayed at one of our best hotels – the Cuillin Hills Hotel. There, over a light meal, lamb sandwiches and a big pot of tea, and as we walked on the lawn and in the woods around, George and I had long discussions. He mentioned that he had been approached by an intelligence agency regarding using contacts to go take a look at – places – but he had declined the offer. He bought an Alpha Technology Mark 2 Interface Unit, which he wanted to show to some rich old lady in Pennsylvania – one of the Mellon family I think. But I heard no more about it.

While in Portree George and his wife came up to Grianan for a cup of tea and more discussions – and they hoped to see this secret laboratory they were sure I had.

I told him of my severe doubts about the authenticity of the Spiricom results but he still believed them to be true – I asked him if he had ever witnessed the Spiricom in operation – the actual lab work was carried out at O'Neill's home in Virginia – as opposed to just getting tapes and reports. He said, yes, he had witnessed it, and indeed had made a video of it – which he would let me see – he mentioned that for the video O'Neill insisted on being filmed from behind – with his back to the camera. I asked, "So – you never actually saw what he did with his hands or if there was a noise-tube leading to his mouth?" He admitted he had not.

I never did see the video.

Until in 2003, thanks to David Monaghan's TV Documentary for Channel 4, the Spiricom Video was shown as part of the program – courtesy of Mark Macy – George Meek's heir apparent.

As you can hear on the tapes there is no time when O'Neill and the contact are <u>speaking at the same time</u>.

Indicating, as I suggested at the time, that O'Neill spoke with his own voice when he was supposed to be saying something, and with noise injected into his mouth for when the contact was speaking.

The give-away, however, is in the body language. Bill O'Neill speaks quite emphatically and, as he does so, there is quite a lot of arm-raising – in fact a bit too much, a bit OTT, as though he was dramatizing the whole thing, acting. But the thing is – and this is really quite sad – you may note that in at least one part of the video, when Doc Mueller is supposed to be speaking, O'Neill's body is doing the body language, just as though O'Neill himself was speaking. (Which I believe he was.)

He is supposed to be silent, listening to Doc speaking – but his arms and upper body are moving in time with Doc's voice. A small and sad point – but the video was only ever made for private viewing by Meek himself.

So....

There are too many strikes against the whole Spiricom business – but each year there are a flock of new true believers.

Well – I was there at the time – I forced the truth about the design to be revealed – I had long discussions with George Meek – and on a personal basis I was quite fond of himself and his wife – but it was all an illusion.

There are those that will never be convinced that it was not all true – but at the end of the day – the proof is in the evidence. Where are the results – lets see it working. The plans exist, people have made it. It is not a high cost item. I quote from Fuller again,

> 'After the Washington conference, Meek had sent out
> the schematics of the Spiricom designs to several

hundred technicians in the United States and beyond. Over a year later, there were still no tangible results.'

And, at this date of writing, <u>nearly a quarter of a century later</u>, there are still no tangible results.

But yet this is held up as the crowning achievement of EVP.

Contrast this with the Alpha system, (described in the next section). Within a couple of months of its first discovery it was leading to rave reviews from users in three countries. But have you ever heard about the Alpha?

So – before we hear anymore about Spiricom lets hear some *results*.

Let me say this – in all this there is no rancor, no professional jealousy, no attempt to disprove EVP or survival – I really am not in any competition with Spiricom.   It is unfortunate that that point has to be made clear.

Believe me – if there had been a two-way communication system to the other world I would have got one. I went 6000 miles to try to get one. And you? But here is the point that gets me. And here we go back to J.G. Fuller's book.

> '... Meek ... sent out ... schematics ... to several hundred technicians .... Over a year later, there were still no ... results.
>
> At the same time, he expanded the activities of the Metascience Foundation.
>
> For the first time since his research began, he realized he would have to seek outside funding so that he could make research grants to those whose work seemed most promising.
>
> One of these was Alex MacRae, the Scottish developer and electronics engineer who helped solve the helium

speech problems for Skylab[23] and the first Air [sic]
Shuttle[24] flight.'

All this was unknown to me. I had a long and expensive
phone call with Fuller when he visited London – I didn't mind
the cost of the call too much as he had promised a signed copy
of his book when it was done.

But it never arrived. I put this down to typical media behavior
– all over you when they need you, but forget you the minute
they are gone.

And then, in a phone conversation about something else, Meek
apologized to me for what had been said about me in Fuller's
book and said he would see that it was taken out of the British
edition.

I wasn't too bothered about any of this, I had got used to
criticism and I hadn't really expected the book, anyway.

What I didn't find out until years later, was this, Fuller again....

> 'By the beginning of 1984, Meek's bloodhound
> persistence began to bring in substantial grants for his
> redesigned Metascience Foundation. One
> organization provided a grant of thirty thousand
> dollars....'[25]

But the most shattering discovery was to find this, many years
later, when at last I got a copy of Fuller's book.

> 'Exited by MacRae's technical approach, Meek visited
> him in Scotland. He went over his work carefully and
> found it to be of great importance. He was so
> delighted with MacRae's progress that when he
> returned home, he arranged to make a major grant

---

[23] Skylab was originally called the MOL (Manned Orbital Laboratory),
designed to carry out experiments in space, it used a mixed Helium/Oxygen
atmosphere aboard.

[24] He means the Space Shuttle - on TV you could see the little box that
resulted from my research, when the Shuttle crew talk to the (then) Vice
President Bush as he congratulates them.

[25] Page 213, 'The Ghost on 29 Megacycles', by J. G. Fuller, Signet, 1981.

---

from his new foundation of five thousand dollars and gave MacRae a hearty endorsement....'[26]

No.

It never happened. Maybe I blinked, causing me to miss the 'hearty endorsement', but the rest is – what is the polite word, begins with an 'f' ... "*fiction.*"

Now I understood why they hadn't wanted me to see a copy of the book!

The unfortunate thing is that for every starry-eyed person who comes in to EVP and is told that Spiricom is "the thing, man" – and who tries it and spends a lot of time on it and gets no results – that is someone *lost* to EVP. They have been betrayed – they have been let down – and all for the sake of somebody's prestige – somebody who wanted to be seen as an expert in EVP.

There is no scientific conspiracy trying to do down EVP – even if there were they wouldn't have to do very much, for we are way too good at doing it ourselves.

For whatever desire to bathe in reflected glory – promoting an unworkable system is as good as sabotaging EVP.

The Case of William O'Neill

Bill O'Neill, in the beginning, before Spiricom, started to actually see and hear his visitors, Doc Nick, Fred and Doc Mueller – you can call them hallucinations if you like – at any rate he went to see a psychiatrist to check with him if he was going crazy, recognizing that these are classic signs of possible schizophrenia.

The psychiatrist was an old friend and the consultation was over a "long-time-no-see" reunion dinner, with his wife present. After hearing the situation – I don't know if it was before the Daiquiris or after the brandies, his friend the psychiatrist replied,

'Bill did I ever say you were crazy?'

---

[26] Page 205, 'The Ghost on 29 Megacycles' by J.G. Fuller, Signet, 1981.

At which, presumably, Bill heaved a great sigh of relief.

It was a neat and diplomatic answer – worthy of "Dr. Frasier Crane" at his smoothest.

Even the author J.G. Fuller writes,[27]

> 'In my recent visit however, I found Bill on the first day to be remote, uncooperative, petty, withdrawn, morose and bitter.'

He continues,

> 'On the second day, while he was working with people at his little healing center, I found him to be charismatic, outgoing, exuberant, confident, and expansive.'

But there is one final comment I would like to include.

At one time, in Northern California, Dr. Wilson van Dusen was Chief Psychiatrist at the Mendocino State Mental Hospital. In a superb bit of lateral thinking – he decided – well, if those guys are hearing voices talking to them – why don't I try to get in touch with the voices through the patients. So he would communicate to the voices using the patient as a sort of messenger – the patient could hear the voices, but Dr. Van Dusen could not.

Among Dr. Van Dusen's discoveries from this cunning bit of research was the fact that among the various voices for the different patients the names "Doc" and "Fred" were prominent. He also came to the conclusion that behind the voices were what could only be called "spirits" – what we earlier referred to as 'Informational parasites.' The Swedenborg Society published a booklet on the subject called 'The Presence of Spirits in Madness.'

It was O'Neill and the voices that were the main sources of the Spiricom – George Meek was the organizer, the financial expert and the promoter – all essential functions – but he was not and never claimed to be the inventor of the Spiricom – that glory belongs to William O'Neill – the forgotten man

---

[27] Page 180, 'The Ghost of 29 Megacycles', J.G. Fuller, Signet, 1981.

behind the scenes. And of course, also, to Fred Ingstrom, Doc Nick and Doc Mueller.

Alpha Technology

During 1982 I had concluded – which was the general viewpoint in EVP at that time, that you had to have mediumistic abilities to be able to get EVP.

I decided to try to make a tester that would show if a person had mediumistic abilities.

Maybe a person could use it in a biofeedback kind of way to try to train himself or herself to develop such abilities.

And so I designed something along the lines of a skin-resistance biofeedback unit. As you relaxed or got tense the tone put out by the unit would rise or fall.

But instead of the usual tone I decided to make it squawk or groan according to whether a person was stressed or relaxed. It would also react very quickly – just to sudden thoughts, almost.

So, one was connected up to this machine like a pulse monitor or lie detector – with thumb pads. But if instead of listening to it direct you allowed the unit to be picked up on a radio then it became extremely sensitive – one could hear one's pulse going swoosh – swoosh – swoosh.

And then it started producing crude voice-like sounds – it was producing EVP!

The method has changed a lot since those days and is now called Alpha Technology and has applications in areas as different as brain monitoring and blood flow detection.

The EVP unit is called the Interface Unit – because it comes between the physical universe and the universe of information and enables one to communicate with the other.

The first discovery was made in late 1982 and six identical units were made up and sent out to 12 selected people for a month each. All got EVP – and so as well as producing results in a volume unmatched by any other system, the Interface Unit proved beyond all doubt that anybody could get EVP – no unusual abilities were required. This upset some people who still regard the IU as an adversary.

If nothing else, the Alpha Technology IU deserves to go down in history for proving that anyone can do EVP. Those who were not around at the time cannot imagine how 'elitist' EVP was at that time.

Thrilled with the good results we were getting, I wrote a short article for the magazine, 'Light.'

But with their next issue I was devastated by the response to my article, it was page after page after page of quite nasty comment.

This did not come from the magazine or from the College of Psychic Studies that published the article. In fact we were awarded the annual Sir Oliver Lodge Medal for our pioneering work in developing EVP or perhaps more accurately – Instrumental Transcommunication (ITC) as it is called in Europe. The pages of vituperation came from the newly formed body called the AAEVP. They were seeking publicity and wanted to put down the competition – as they saw it. I almost gave up at that point, for good.

The IU has gone through some transformations since then and is now not currently available except to full-time researchers as the V.7 (Mk 4) and using an entirely different technology. There will be examples of voices obtained with recent Alpha Technology on the CD, and some of the examples quoted here are of that recent type.

The latest technology enables us to pick up "threaded" communications – voice samples where one is linked in some way to the next, as when one voice comments on what another has just said. I believe that threaded communications will be a major feature of future research

This too is unique to us, except for possibly the work of Dr. Anabela Cardoso, publisher of the ITC Journal,[28] an excellent Journal about EVP, which has an impressive list of subscribers, and sets a very high standard.

_____

[28] ITC JOURNAL, Calle Carral 23 bajo, 36202 - Vigo - Pontevedra - Spain

Delegates at the Journal of ITC Congress in Vigo, Spain, in April 2004, photo Carlos Fernandez

To read reports of the experiments we have done at Skyelab, and other articles – some quite technical – I invite you to visit the website WWW.skyelab.co.uk.

If you want to read about the Alpha story in more detail read the article in Fate Magazine by former Alpha user Dr. Jose Feola. There is a link to that Fate magazine article on the website mentioned above. Professor Feola also had an article about the Alpha published in the Spanish journal "Enigmas." In spite of all this the AAEVP banned the article he wrote for their quarterly magazine on the grounds that it did not accord with their objectives.

Other Alpha (Mk 3) users included Professor Charl Vorster of the Dept. of Psychology at the Rand University in South Africa and Sarah Estep of the American Association for the Electronic Voice Phenomenon.

Although he never used it, George Meek also purchased a Mk 2 Alpha to show to the old lady in Pennsylvania, from whom he was seeking support for his foundation.

EVPMaker (Stefan Bion)

One of the early EVP pioneers in Germany was Fidelio Koberle, Dip. Psych. Some time ago Koberle came up with the idea – what if we sliced up a piece of speech into its component parts and then mixed them up at random?

Essentially this is a variation on the methods of Babble, Porridge, and all the way back to Bonner's multiple voice mixture. This is good science – with the torch being handed on from one to the next – each person striving to do their best.

But to do what Koberle wanted is no easy matter – it would need someone pretty good with computer technology and such a one was Stefan Bion.

He developed a software package that will run on Windows

that he called EVPMaker. And extraordinary though it may seem – it works!

The world of EVP/ITC should congratulate Mr. Bion and Dr. Koberle on their achievement.

Stefan Bion

Perhaps the foremost researcher using EVPMaker at present is Professor JA Martinez.

Here are some details of his work.

J.A.Martinez (Ph.D. in Philosophy, University of California, 1980), is an emeritus faculty member of San Diego State University, and has been researching the

Dr Martinez

EVP since the fall of the year 2002 using Stefan Bion's EVPMaker.

He has obtained what appear to be anomalous results, particularly, once he was able, with the aid of the program **Cool Edit**, to significantly reduce the interference of the random flow of sounds produced by the chopped phonemes generated by **EVPMaker.**

According to Stefan Bion these meaningless phonemes are the basis of the digital /sonic manifestation of EVP. Dr. Martinez believes these anomalous preliminary findings, should be at this time, free of New Age metaphysical assumptions and of definite philosophical conclusions, and should spur the scientific community to seriously evaluate research in a field that has been unjustifiably neglected in recent times.

Dr. Martinez, in the past, formed part of the editorial staff of **Cognition and Brain Theory,** a journal devoted to publishing papers in the fields of philosophy, psychology, linguistics, artificial intelligence and neuroscience. His academic research concerned the nature of mind and cognition and its physical implementation in the brain. This involved him in a number of areas, including the philosophy of representation, and of perception in general; theoretical neuroscience; the semantics of natural languages, and metaphysics. (The mind-body problem)

Lack of satisfaction with extant theories of the mind have disposed him to be receptive to the study of EVPs as an area of study of paraphysics where rigorous, research endeavors , such as those of Alexander MacRae, a pioneer in the scientific approach to the [problem], have begun to command the attention of the international community of scientists interested in the nature of the mind and its relationship to the body.

Dr. Martinez is doing interesting work into binary responses – trying to get a Yes or NO answer – which brings us back to "raps" and the Fox sisters, (in case of confusion – no, the Fox Sisters are not a Rap group – they were the gals who invented spiritualism 150 years ago!)

With EVPMaker what you do is you record a piece of speech and then you set the system to chop that up into thin (time) slices which then get randomized. One or two things to look out for with EVPMaker.

You may not notice it physically, but it is hard on the ears internal detection mechanism – so play it quietly – and don't use it too much. Make sure it is not overloading and try to keep the slices "thin" – under 100 ms – thick slices just leave significant portions of the original speech as they were and such a piece of speech from the original may be mistaken for EVP.

EVP has come a long way since 1958 – but in all that time there have been only three advances that came from within the EVP field, one is Alpha Technology, plus the use of reverberation and Delta technology; the next is McKee-Estep's reversed speech; and the other is the Koberle-Bion EVPMaker.

The other aspects – Noise Reduction Software, and recorders with psycho-acoustic circuitry, have come from outside the field. Even the publicity circus that is upon us at the time of writing this, stems from Hollywood's version of EVP rather than from anything from within the EVP field.

In all this, EVPMaker presents the greatest intellectual challenge – and the key, if we can ever find it, to a new type of technology.

In the next chapter we will take a look at another method, and the extraordinary claim that "the 12 greatest brains in the world" were working on the problem of EVP – and the triumphant declaration that the answer was "software."

So – what happened next? Don't hold your breath....

Chapter Ten

The Way Ahead

Now that we see a great and growing interest in EVP at last, it is time to take stock of what has been happening – recognizing our mistakes, correcting our course, and envisioning what could happen in the future.

One big question we must look at immediately.

Why in the biggest developed country in the world, with more technology and more religious diversity than anywhere else has EVP failed to take off?

In Germany the VTF – their EVP society – has had 14,000 members.

Brasil has something like 900 members.

Italy is very active, with the biggest array of top-class talent of any country, involved.

But in the UK, USA, France and Japan there is almost no activity.

The American Association for EVP began with 200 members – today, May 2004, 22 years on, almost, there are still around 200 members. Something is not right. Here you have one of the most exciting technical developments in modern history and yet the number of people involved in it in the top technological country in the world is tiny and not growing.

We should look into this.

The AAEVP was begun in 1982 by Sarah Estep – whose book we will refer to later on.

The Association is now managed jointly by Tom and Lisa Butler and the range of its activities is expanding year by year. Their website is AAEVP.com.

They are to hold a convention in Reno Nevada in June 2004.

In the UK and Ireland things are even worse. At one time the technological center for EVP research was the UK and Ireland, with well-defined strategies and Faraday Cage experiments being done. There was particularly strong support from some members of the Roman Catholic clergy and from Irish Radio and Television. Now there seems to be nothing. A former journalist is said to be running things in the UK, but emails just bounce back or are never replied to, reports of new developments are snapped up and credited elsewhere.

Altogether a weird and rather sick scene.

The "Experts"

And Japan seems also to be a disaster area. So far as I can tell there is one person who is really active there, and here is a page from his site. It is actually a copy of information put out by the Brazil group.

> 'On September 3rd 1998, Sonia, a Brazilian researcher, made the first experiment for recording images. She avoided the use of a TV Tube according to the suggestion of a scientist. These are the equipments used:
>
> - Cathode-ray tube with electrostatic deflection
>
> - High stabilized power supply
>
> - Horizontal wave: Sawtooth with a variable length
>
> - Vertical wave: Free aerial input
>
> - Z-axis: Fixed for maximum emission
>
> - External influence: Upon vertical axis input'

Far from being the description of some exotic and specially designed equipment – the above is the description of a common laboratory instrument used in many applications – it is called an oscilloscope. And it uses a Cathode-ray tube – or "CRT" as we generally refer to it. If this is unfamiliar to you check with your nearest electronics or science person. Even a TV repairman should know - although he may be more familiar with the later type of displays such as LCD - Liquid Crystal Display.

It looks as though Sonia, who is not an electronics person - and that is no fault, was a victim of the old "BS baffles brains" scam.

And here, from another site, is the rest of that story which originated from the Brasil group.

> 'These set of equipments avoids the use of a TV Tube, so that people could NOT say that images could have come from any terrestrial TV-station. That's an improvement, as using the cathode-ray tube it is impossible to attract any image emitted on Earth (from TVs stations or Cable TVs) because the range of frequency is completely different.'

This sort of thing makes a genuine electronics person - you don't have to be even a half-way expert - despair, and want to find another planet! A TV tube *is* a CRT. A TV tube is a *CRT*. A *TV* tube is a CRT!

Unless one has a Plasma or LCD screen then every TV uses a cathode ray tube. A TV tube is a Cathode Ray Tube! Don't believe me – check with your nearest TV repairman. Anyone with the slightest pretense of technical knowledge would know this.

In God's name how can we expect anyone to take EVP seriously when statements like the above are promoted all over the Internet? And if you dare to criticize .... wooooo, you're in doo-doo-land.

How can we expect anyone – apart from the most uneducated and gullible – to take EVP seriously with this sort of promotion going on.

Here is the last bit of the quote,

> 'So, any images coming from the tube should have no risk of fake or terrestrial influence. Sonia recorded for one minute directly to the computer (from the tube to the PC via camera). There were more than 1,300 frames to be checked. The first selected frame seemed interesting: it was a Teddy Bear. And

included the following story:

> When Sonia perceived a face of a Teddy Bear in the image she thought it was something very strange. What could be the meaning of it?'

So – what you have is an oscilloscope and pointing at its (CRT) screen you have a video camera.

Once again, the absence of even rudimentary technical knowledge is flagrantly displayed.

What a video camera does is *format* whatever it sees in one of the main *TV* formats. If therefore there is some blur on the CRT screen due to pick up at the Y input of local TV signals, then occasionally at least the video camera formatting will be in sync with the CRT display and will produce a picture or sufficient large scale features to enable the scene to be interpreted as a picture of something.

For those of you who are not technical let me assure you that this is not the description of some new specialized equipment designed to provide EVP TV – although that is what these Web Pages leads one to believe.

These web pages are as good as a big neon sign saying 'No Scientists Here!'

It is as good as a ban on technically qualified people getting into EVP.

What is being described is just a common laboratory instrument called an oscilloscope - with the pretense that this is something new, exotic and terribly hi tech. In actual fact the oscilloscope came on the market some 70 years ago!

One of the problems is that EVP is *full* of supposed "electronic experts." But they are not. We are all too tolerant of this type of put-on. These experts are hi-fi shop owners, draftsmen, technicians and the like - who see in this the chance to play the part of a technical guru. You get them all the time - their main aim in life seems to be to try to impress you.

It is possible that the above-mentioned description came from some technician or other in Brazil posing as an expert and misleading Sonia and everybody else.

The trouble is that there are not enough technically trained people to spot these misleading statements.

Sonia does not have sufficient technical knowledge to be able to concoct the above misleading description – she was misled.

I am not holding up the technically literate person as in some way more desirable – but when you are dealing with a technical subject, and research, then that is the sort of person one wants!

Otherwise one is back to the old principle of the loudest voice commands the most attention. EVP is not – or should not be, a shouting match – but at present it is a running sewer of technical misinformation, a car-boot sale of feuding factions purveying bad information. And charging for it too. I see on the web a ten (10) page booklet about 'secret EVP protocols' [*my backside*] being sold for $10!!! (Download price).

There is no scientific conspiracy aimed at suppressing EVP – what destroys the support it could and should be getting from scientists is the pseudo-science that is promoted through the presence in EVP of self-appointed experts who are not.

This is not a condemnation of one person or another – it is a statement of the obvious – if one posts up on display pseudo-scientific statements pretending that they refer to EVP then one should expect consequences.

EVP at this time is in the hands off the promoters – Raudive was a great promoter, as was Meek, Palmer, and their successors. They are out there even yet – and when it comes time for the communications media to seek out an authority on the subject it is to the promoters that they go.

For the sake of the future, those in EVP who are scientists or scientifically minded should ensure that *our* voices are heard too.

This book is not old pals' reunion book. It is going to alienate some people. Fine. But I care more about the subject than one person's outrage at the truth being exposed.

It looks as though it is the Catholic countries is where EVP has done best, but not so well in non-Catholic countries.

In my view, having been used and spat out several times by various "Foundations", I do not believe that the Foundation is the way forward for EVP.

Sometimes the Foundation is simply a vehicle for the self-aggrandizement of the principal(s) concerned, and its support and communications tend to be confined to a small clique.

In the land of the free it used to be the headlines would read **'Local Boy Makes Good!'** Now the headlines would read **'Local Boy Starts Tax-free Foundation.'**

The morality of some foundations is also questionable – the soliciting and procurement of donations is not a fit means of support for a new science – nor indeed for any science.

There is however another model that we can follow. And as it happens I have seen it happen from its earliest beginnings to its present worldwide role.

I am talking about the home computer, or PC. This has raised communications and the acquiring of knowledge to levels that would otherwise be impossible. It has provided a huge and ever-growing number of skilled and pleasant jobs increasing the self-esteem and financial situation of those involved. It is bringing depressed and difficult economies like those of the giants China and India into some affluence – raising the standard of living and life expectation of their peoples. It generates huge cash flows and has enabled those with the ideas and persistence to build a new life in ways that would be otherwise impossible.

If you go back to the early days – it began with something that a guy in Japan had invented called a "micro-processor".

These were small 4-bit devices of limited usefulness – but people in the know could see their vast potential.

In the beginning, engineers from all over the states and abroad would come to the Bay Area of San Francisco (soon to become known as Silicon Valley) to attend lectures and do courses and buy books about these strange new devices called micro-processors.

Fortunately, some people who could look ahead more than most put money into the small start-up companies that were growing up beside established giants – like little acorns beside great oak trees.

And gradually it all expanded and expanded – from strange little devices that were not much use except for studying, the micro-processor became the micro-computer, and the micro-computer became the Personal Computer, and the Personal Computer became the PC, and the PC became the Home Computer or laptop or work–station...

And that is the route that EVP could follow.

There is another model that is probably just as successful and that is medicine. The good thing about medicine is that it is based on a code of ethics and it requires a dedication and discipline equal to that required of the engineer.

In this model the personnel would be closer in their practices to engineers, but in their organization more like the medical practitioners. But note – the fancy instrumentation a medical facility has nowadays came from the engineers, not the medical doctors.

Get honest. Get real. Get the knowledge and the technology out to the people – all the people – not just a special few.

I read a rather neat (cool) thing on the Net some years ago – it said,

> 'You are not a human being having a spiritual experience – you are a spirit having a human experience.'

You do not need to be a spiritualist to be a spirit – <u>you already are one</u>.

You do not need to burn incense or be born of a gypsy to be psychic – you already are.

The time that is coming will see our existence opening up into new dimensions beyond our wildest dreams.

The informational universe is not somebody's special abode – it is your Inheritance and it is your Home. It – it would seem – is where you came from and to which you will return.

Life in the physical is an interlude – some say it is just a Celestial Video Game.

Death is the prompt that tells you, 'GAME OVER.'

However, if we take away the shades of superstition, the ever-so profitable shades of superstition, there is no such actual thing as death.

As we shall presently see.

Chapter Eleven

Death – the Truth

There isn't a black cloud of bad stuff called Death, out there, waiting for you.

There isn't some Black Presence out there waiting for the time when "your number is up."

People do not die of death.

There is no such thing as death.

Let's go to a funeral parlor, look at a body. Open a coffin – and point to some death.

Point. No – that's not death there in the coffin.

What is there in that coffin is a non-functional body.

Hospitals are full of non-functional bodies. But in that coffin is a special case. It is a non-functional body that has got beyond repair.

There was no one around smart enough to fix it.

And so it was put in a wooden box and buried in the ground. This – as the top species of evolution, on this the most advanced planet in the Universe (being, as you know, the only inhabited one) – is how we do it. We is Homo Sapiens - we is Top Dogs!

We put the bodies we can't fix in boxes and bury them in the ground.

Woof woof.

Until very recently, even in the advanced National Health Service in the UK, the average doctor in general practice had less technology available to him than the average TV repairman. You see the priorities?

You dont die of death, you die of lack of sufficient medical competence to prevent it.

In the mid-1800s, the average life expectancy was around 39.

By the beginning of the twentieth century the life expectancy was noticeably longer – largely due to advances in medical knowledge and practice – including public hygiene, anesthetics and antiseptics.

It wasn't that Death had taken a holiday – there never was anything called Death.

And the average life expectancy has risen, and risen – up until the present – thanks to medical advances.

Instead of failing to be able to do any more when the patient was 39 we now fail to be able to do anymore when the patient is 72 or whatever. And that is progress.

It is not Death that has moved – it is medical technology.

We can now live with malfunctions that would have been fatal in years past.

Getting old – aging – is simply the accumulation of malfunctions.

The body is a vehicle for living in the physical universe.

You can feel with it, you can see with it, you can hear with it – you can move around with it – you can join in games with it – a superb piece of equipment.

When a body gets beyond repair its a sad thing – but why?

There is nothing special about the atoms that make it up. The calcium atoms in your late Uncle Mortimer's teeth were in a cow's udder a few months earlier. The iron atoms in his blood were in the backside of a bull. There is nothing special about the atoms in one body as compared with another. So – what is it?

It is what the atoms add up to. The patterns the shapes, the sounds – and what all these things are is information – the information that is in the eye of the beholder, or in the ear of the listener – this is mind-to-mind communication – via atoms.

It is not the calcium atoms that wear-out, or the iron atoms that wear-out, it is always just a systems problem.

The body is a system composed of various sub-systems composed of sub-sub systems – and so on, all the way down to the basic system – the cell.

System failures lead to the body becoming non-operational. The basic failure may lie at the cellular level – the various forms of cancer lie at that level.

The heart, the pumping system, is also a common type of malfunction – but we are getting better at handling that one.

The blood chemical distribution system – blocked arteries and that sort of thing is another problem area.

The religionists have latched on to the presence of a malfunction beyond repaired (MBR) – "Death" as they call it – is one of their areas of expertise – the transfer from this life to the next.

They have also latched on to the other area of transfer – from prior state to physical life – "Birth."

And to complete the area dominance they have latched onto the pre-birth or body procurement area – "Marriage."

They invest the whole thing with ceremonies and decoration and above all see to the emotional needs of those affected.

Which is good.

What happens as a consequence of MBR is the cutting-off of communication; and the rapid deterioration of the forms of the body due to the vulnerability of biological construction.

The cutting-of of communication is what is the greatest loss to those related to the deceased.

It may be that EVP will develop along the lines of being able to facilitate some continuing of this communication – although there are injunctions against doing this. For example the Bible forbids it – but the problem seems to have been more with fraudulent mediums than any big problem with the practice as such.

However, the Bible is the book of the Hebrews and in the Jewish religion there is no afterlife anyway, so anyone saying they could contact the dead was pretty obviously in conflict with the religion of the people.

But those adhering to the Biblical injunction against trying to contact the deceased are not alone in trying to condemn this.

Yogi Ramacharaka[29] writing in 'Fourteen Lessons in Yogi Philosophy and Oriental Occultism'[30] has this to say,

> 'But before going any further, let us stop for a moment to say that both the sinking into the restful state, and the soundness and continuance of it may be interfered with by those left in the earth-life. A soul which has "something on its mind" to communicate, or which is grieved by the pain of those left behind (especially if it hears the lamentations and constant call for its return) will fight off the dreamy state creeping over it, and will make desperate efforts to return.'

He continues,

> 'These half-awake souls often manifest in spiritualist circles.'

And,

> 'We should avoid delaying the progress of those who have passed on, by our selfish demands — let them sleep on and rest, awaiting the hour of their transformation.'

This final quote is also interesting.

> [The soul] passes immediately to the plane in the Astral World [Informational Universe] for which it is fitted and to which it is drawn by the Law of Attraction.

[The force of attraction is dealt with later in this Chapter.]

---

[29] The pen name adopted by Baba Barata and William Walker Atkinson as co-authors.

[30] L.N. Fowler &Co. Ltd., 1201/3 Chadwell Heath Rd., Romford, Essex, UK.RM6 4DH.

Now the Astral World, in all of its stages and planes, is not a place but a state, as we have before stated.'

I mention that last quote to show that this is not a case of my airing the views of some Yogi people, these people have credentials, in the realm of the investigators of the Beyond – those who actually get out there and do it, as opposed to those who simply write about it, or who have Important Opinions to be aired - this person, Baba Barata - has "street cred."

Emmanuel Swedenborg, from his researches, remarked that time in Heaven was not like time as we know it but was a state and change of state – what we call a 'scan.'

Let me quote a little from "Far Journeys" by Robert A. Monroe. This is a transcript from an Explorer Session - these are deliberately controlled out of the body experiences. The Explorer is the person doing the session.

To begin with there are some preceding remarks by Monroe.

'In speaking to the Explorer, the being [encountered by the Explorer] is limited in vocabulary to that in the memory bank of said Explorer. Therefore it often shows hesitation in searching for the correct word to express what needs to be described....'

Well now, that is just what Swedenborg reported centuries before, and isn't that possibly why the EVP utterances that one gets relate to one's native language.

Another statement against trying to contact the dead are the followers of Agni Yogi – the Yoga of Wisdom. What they say is that we are all evolving and it would be wrong to affect someone who once lived with us in our time on Earth, by trying to stay in touch with them when they had moved on – to an area we cant comprehend, and another life with its own new lessons to be learned.

What these people seem to be suggesting is that *death is a system*.

Nevertheless this often sudden cutting-off of communication due to MBR leaves a sorely hurting emptiness in a person's life – an emptiness that may have unfortunate mental and physical effects in years to come.

Our primitive state of understanding does not help.

The calcium and iron atoms of the person's body do not cease to exist – what goes is our contact with the form that the atoms were organized into.

Information does not die – it is not of the physical universe. Dying is a feature of the physical universe resulting from serial time. Dying is not a natural and inevitable event – except in a universe that contains serial time, and a planet that has bodies which wear out and are difficult to repair.

Dying is a side-effect of serial time. It is not even a very important side-effect – except that to us, in our primitive state, it is upsetting.

Meanwhile coffee is being made, children are eating ice-cream, the sun is shining, doctors are trying to repair malfunctioning physical systems without the tools to do the job and not enough information to be able to understand what is going on.

Side-effects of the running of serial time.

Information is not subject to serial time. Let us now take a look at the very big subject of Information and New Dimensions.

Chapter Twelve

Information Space

Five hundred years ago there was a king in England named Henry the Eighth. Among his many other activities he wrote a song called 'Greensleeves.'

It has an instantly recognizable tune. It does not matter whether you are listening to it coming from a radio, or on a CD, or tape, or it is the Mormon Tabernacle Choir singing it in some grand hall, or if it is just someone humming it as they wash dishes in their kitchen in a house in Melbourne Australia – the time, the place, the physical circumstances do not matter – the tune – the information – is still the same.

And it didn't decay with the passing of the last 600 years to become some other tune, or to become just a bunch of random sounds. It was unaffected by the passing of time.

In ancient Greece, thousands of years ago, there was a philosopher and mathematician called Pythagoras – and one of his most famous writings concerned a triangle. So, Pythagoras drew a triangle and explained what it was to his students.

Today, in Moscow, in New York, in Tokyo – all over the world, teachers are drawing triangles for their students. And the students all hate this. But the form – the information – is still the same. A triangle has not decayed into a small ball of lines going nowhere – a triangle is still a triangle – it is not affected by place or time – a triangle in Tokyo today is the same as a triangle in Athens three thousand years ago.

Information is unaffected by serial time. Serial time is the time that keeps running on in the physical universe – the time that began with the Big Bang[31] and continues on and on and on, relentlessly.

---

[31] This time was actually produced by the ejection velocity of information from the White Hole. Velocity of information flow, or rate of change of information, is what we call 'the passage of time' or just "time."

It is the time shown by the movement of the hands on your clock face, or the changing of the digits.

In the informational dimensions there is no serial time it is eternal. You get time, but it is a result of scanning – like a track on a CD player. Consider a compact disc – a CD. That is packed with information but to experience any of it you have to scan it.

This can be done in one of two ways. You spin the disk and a tiny light and a tiny "eye" watch the track as it goes by. This way you pick up a stream of information and the stream gets converted into sounds you can hear. The other way would be for the disk to stay still and for the light and eye to scan the track by moving along it. This too generates a time sequence of notes – the sort of thing that we call music.

A CD is actually quite a good illustration of a little information universe.

So, in the big information universe time – change – is generated by scanning.

In the same way that you could regard your life in the physical universe as the track that you are playing at the moment – so there are any number of tracks which can be played in the big informational universe

The way that you kow where you are in the physical universe is by location. That big mountain is three miles to the west of me, the sea is 100 yards in front and the smaller hill is 1 mile to the southeast – that locates me. You locate yourself by reference. I am just north of San Francisco, I am in central Madrid – but however your location is described by references, it is always "here". To you your location is "here" – to me *my* location is "here." In the physical universe locations are in space. And the more similar that your 'here' is to my 'here' the closer we are.

Jack and Jill are talking on their cellular phones.

Jill, 'I am at The Pier – where are you?'

Jack, 'I am just approaching The Pier now. But I can't see you yet. Where exactly are you?'

Jill, 'Over by the Harbor Bar, just to the left.'

Jack, 'Of course – I see you now!'

And soon both share "here" as closely as possible.

In the informational universe one is located by thought. If one is thinking about polar bears one is in the polar bear area. If one is thinking about Mars one is in the Mars area.

In the information universe there is neither serial time nor space made up of locations.

In the informational universe – and remember you can call it the spiritual universe if you prefer – what we are talking about is the sort of thing reported by Robert Monroe and other Out-Of-The-Body-Experiencers, and who should you believe, some aged expert who has studied the books of the Hebrews for 140 years and wears black and white clothes to prove it – or people who have actual informational-universe experience?

In the informational universe the rule is – similarity equals closeness – but not closeness as in physical terms.

There is no physical space in the informational universe. You dont have to travel from one region another to get from Polar Bears to Mars – you just think, and without time or effort you are where you intend to be.

Almost all explorers have mentioned this feature of the Informational Universe. Raymond Moody the well-known Near Death Experience (NDE) expert mentions one of his subjects as describing it like a huge library where all knowledge is stored according to its nature.

A well-known Sci-Fi writer, when reportedly having a Near Death Experience, described it as being like an endless smorgasbord with all knowledge laid out before him.

The thing with the Information Universe is that you can view it in different ways.

You can view it as Information Space, or I-space as it is more usually called. Information is not space in the sense of physical universe distance space.

But among many other things I-space contains Information about space and so viewing a scene in I-space will contain apparent space – just as real as physical universe distance space – but it is "just" information – not distance. It is information about space – not space itself. Recall in your mind a picture of your kitchen. That is information about your kitchen – it is not your kitchen itself. Yet the space in your picture looks just like space. Indeed, in some circumstances your experience of the information can be just as real as the experience of the information that comes via your body's sensory channels.

Looking at physical space you also see "just" information – but to see *another space* – say Sicily – you would have to physically *go* to an airport and get on a physical plane so that you can actually be there and see there.

In Information Space – everything looks just as it does in "reality" and if you want to see Sicily – its there, all around you. You didn't even have to move.

Of course, to play out the reality aspect, you could *see* yourself going to the airport and going on the plane and flying and eventually *arriving* at Palermo or wherever.

Which would be more like real life.

So – it is like a real existence – taking real to mean the same as in the physical universe, even though our definition of reality – scientifically – lacks something.

For example, imagine that you have taken a picture of outside your house – the space outside your house – then the picture will look as though it has that space in it – but it is just information.

Take a block of modeling clay. Toss a coin. If it comes up Heads model the clay into the form of an eagle, if it is Tails, model it into the form of a butterfly. Two different things. But scientifically there is no difference. Whether the shape comes out as that of a butterfly or an eagle is irrelevant. So long as it still weighs the same and all the original atoms are still there, nothing has happened. That is because science is substance science – it deals only with materiality.

It is only when you include the informational aspects – the shapes – the form, not just the substance – that you are dealing with *reality*.

Scans, Time Tracks and Episodes of Experience

A section of Informational Universe can be viewed and it will look just as though what one was seeing was a part of the physical universe.

You can do a scan – basically that is what living is, doing a scan – and experience an information flow.

What we like is a good flow of experience. For the moment, TV soaps are the best we can do in that respect. Primitive – but its still only the 21st Century, and these are backward times.

You can do a scan of an section of the Informational Universe and in the information flow be walking down the main street of a sea-side town, people smiling to you as you go by, and an Ice Cream Parlor just ahead, which is where you are going.

And it is eternal.

You can go back there and (because serial time does not exist) it will be as though it is the first – fresh – walking down the main street of a sea-side town, people smiling to you as you go by, and an Ice Cream Parlor just ahead, which is where you are going.

And you can go back again and it will be as though it is the first – fresh – walking down the main street of a sea-side town, people smiling to you as you go by, and an Ice Cream Parlor just ahead, which is where you are going.

Or you can do a scan and in the information flow be entering a great garden with gently tinkling fountains and people walking slowly through the trees, in twos and threes, discussing meanings and who made them.

And you can do it again, as though you had never experienced it before, and in it be entering a great garden with gently tinkling fountains and people walking slowly through the trees, in twos and threes, discussing meanings and who made them.

The stuff doesn't wear out. It is not the material world, like here.

The TV program "The Twilight Zone" did quite nice portrayals of this sort of thing. Very liberating. In this case though it is the Daylight Zone – there is nothing "spooky" about it unless you choose to have "spookiness" in it and call informational beings "spirits" and be overawed by what they do, and call them "paranormal powers."

OK – that's one way of looking at it, experiencing it through playing "tracks" – its like playing tracks on a CD – except with a CD each track is a different piece of Music, whereas in this case each "track" is a different Life, or even just an episode – like a Life clip or sample track.

See your travel agent. (Only joking. Didn't mean to scare you.)

Where troubles can begin is if "ersatz"[32] I-space is involved. There is real I-space, and there is this pseudo I-space, which consists of *memories* of experience, forming a little information track of their own, with sequential time as an added dimension.

You can also look at I-space as a whole ... endless, eternal –the repository of all information – like a CD whose size is beyond imagining.

A Consideration of Scale

Imagine a CD as big as the Sahara desert, stretching from the Atlantic in the west to the Nile in the East – like an endless mirror, glittering with flashes of iridescent color in the blazing sun.

And imagine a tiny ant trying to cross it – from West to East. Day after day, week after week, month after month, on its tiny feet, it walks on.

Then one day, stopping for a moment to rest, it looks down and there beside its tiny front right foot there is a little defect on the surface of the Sahara-wide CD – a tiny pit, almost too small to see.

---

[32] Ersatz - fake, imitation, manufactured, synthetic.

That, in comparing scales, would be the physical universe.

Calling I-space "The Other Side" – as though it was a mirror image of Earth, is vanity beyond vanity.

This little black hole, this pit in the surface, this microscopic vortex is where we live.

Information is not subject to decay, it does not wear out. Substance – the stuff of the physical universe – decays and wears out. It is subject to change - the spin that we call time.

Death of Functionality

When a person dies – when their systems get beyond being repaired by the technology of our time, then the substance can no longer support the form – the organization – that is that body. A body is organized chemicals.

And gradually, with time, that organization will decay and be no more.

So there are two deaths – the operational death – when there is cessation of communication and activity, a funeral and mourning.

At this point there is still flesh and blood and eyes on the body. It is still an organization of substances. Gradually, (with the exception of the skeleton) that organization decays and is no more.

Except for one thing – that organization is *information*, it is form not substance. The substance undergoes chemical change, and thus "decays" as we call it – but the organization is information and that does not decay.

This "organization body" – information without substance – is perhaps what is promised in the New Testament –a body that shall arise and be incorruptible in the last days – and shall live forever.

From Corinthians 1, Chapter 15, regarding the body that is buried and the body hereafter.

> '44 It is sown a natural body; it is raised a spiritual body. There is a natural body, and there is a spiritual body.

[53] For this corruptible must put on incorruption, and this mortal must put on immortality.

[54] So when this corruptible shall have put on incorruption, and this mortal shall have put on immortality, then shall be brought to pass the saying that is written, Death is swallowed up in victory.

[55] O death, where is thy sting? O grave, where is thy victory?'

If we bring it down to the language of our age, for that was first written in another age, and for another culture, in our language what we are talking about is the change from a time-dominated zone to a time-free zone.

It is time that causes corruption (decay, rotting); and it is timelessness that allows incorruption (no decay, no rotting).

Life Everlasting

This "organization body" – information without substance – is also, exactly, the description of a ghost.

A limited life span is something that could only occur in serial time. Time goes on, a body is born, time goes on, the body grows and multiplies, time goes on, the body decays and is no more.

In the Informational Universe life everlasting is the norm – death is an oddity that could only occur 'way down there in the physical, down the black hole.

Life everlasting is such a normal feature that it probably does not need a special name.

Would you say, "Oh – look at the cat with the tail?"

Or simply, "Oh – look at the cat?"

Life everlasting is just Life, just as a Cat with a tail is just a Cat.

OK – there are exceptions – a Manx cat has no tail and in the physical universe life is ended by Death – weird, but true. Let me qualify that, in the physical universe <u>on planet Earth in the</u> <u>21st Century</u>, life is terminated by death.

You really can't avoid life everlasting. The physical Universe religionists – who are really like ticket touts outside a football stadium on the day of the Big Match – will tell you,

"Do dis an' do dat – an' boom-boom-boom – we see you get Life Everlasting. So give us your money. Now."

But what if you already have a ticket?

And what if the biggest line of customers around the block (metaphorically speaking) is for Schazzam Travel Agents, 'Don't be Jaded – get In–Carnated!'

Get a body and experience Life
Not Everlasting – Guaranteed – a
genuine life with problems,
unexpected failures, time
running out, death and a sad
funeral! Real Passion – gut-
wrenching experience. The Thrill
of your Everlasting Life!

Get de–jaded today!

Freedom of Belief

One thing about Information Space – anything is possible. One could even be as narrow-minded and commonsensical as one felt like being. There – freedom of belief is reality, it is as solid a feature of the place as the sunlit path on your morning walk through The Park.

At this time, here, beliefs tended to be treated as though they were statements about physical reality, supported by truth.

People will compare one person's belief with another's, "Yes, but his is an unsupported belief – there is no evidence for it."

A belief is just a belief – it is not a statement of fact. There is, fundamentally, total freedom of belief. One can believe anything.

It may be considered true – in the sense that it corresponds to physical reality – or it may be considered untrue, in the sense that it does not correspond to physical reality. But either way does not make it any less a belief. A belief should not be considered as either true or untrue. True and untrue refer to conforming or not conforming to physical reality.

There can be true statements and untrue statements but these terms do not apply to belief.

Where problems arise it is where a belief is treated as though it was a statement, either by the believer or by someone else.

You can believe anything you want – but just don't confuse it with being real or being unreal. This is how many people involved in psychic activities get in trouble. They confuse a belief with physical reality.

There is a place where all beliefs are "true" and that is the Information Universe.

The Basic Law of Information

As you know, location in the Information Universe is determined by thought – and so similarity becomes "closeness". It is like the way that all the books on gardening in the library are side-by-side in the same section. The librarian is just following the rules of information space. The library is organized that way because it is trying to mirror the properties of information – the logic of I-space. It is a mapping of the way that I-space is organized, making it possible for us to walk around and find what we are looking for.

In the past one application of this law was called Sympathetic Magic.

Chapter Thirteen

Heaven and Hell

Due to the fundamental rules of I-space, there tends to be a region where all is *good* – where all the *good* things are.

And adjoining that there would be an area where things are *quite* good – OK – but not as good as in the good things place.

And adjoining that good things place – on "the other side" is a place where the *best* things are to be found.

So, what you get throughout the Information Universe is a polarization with total *good* at one pole and total *bad* at the other. And that reads as Heaven and Hell, with a Total Bad to Total Good gradient in between.

It is also a road map of I-space telling you how to get there. If you are yourself *good* then you will tend to re-locate to Heaven. If you are yourself *bad* then you will tend to relocate to Hell.

The marvelous thing is the Christian Intervention. By forgiveness your slate is wiped clean.

And so there is a distribution of informational beings, with the ill-intended tending to favor the Bad areas and the well-intended tending to favor the Good areas – unlike what happens in the physical universe, where it is the laws of space and time that determine where things are.

In I-space you would not expect your pleasant little seaside town (for example) to be invaded by Hell's Angels. Similarly you would not expect a Black Sabbath to be invaded by family people in sun-hats eating ice-cream.

The top Swedish Scientist Emmanuel Swedenborg wrote about all this, although not quite in these words, four Centuries ago. Of course he also got quite a lot wrong and played to his audience, so he is not the most reliable of sources.

One thing we should be aware of – though it will not be popular to say so – is that one man's Heaven is another man's "Yeah – very nice – but its not quite what I had in mind."

Heaven should not be thought of as a uniformity – but as having many areas – in my Father's House are many Mansions......

What you get here, down in the pit, however, are the religionists all competing with each other, insisting that they are right and thus everyone else is wrong, like a bunch of cut-throat real estate agents, each trying to sell its own bit of the holiday beaches and telling you there are no other bits.

As we consider the truth that is the existence of EVP and as we try to work out what is beyond in terms of new dimensions the time will surely come when wars and conflict based on the worship of religion will surely cease.

The problem, you see, is not with the teachings, nor their source – but with the religionists *who worship their religion,* and thereby commit idolatry – for that was what idolatry was – the worship of the statues and the formalities of attending to them, in sum, the worship of a religion.

The primary function of religion, it would seem, is decorative. Whether in Tokyo or Seville giant statues are carried through the thronged streets by sweating young men to great applause.

Innocent fun?

War

Wars were fought and the Christian Church split apart by conflict as to which day the Festival of Easter should be on – more decoration.

War is not a normal way of doing things except with us. The time will come when people will wonder what kind of people we were to accept War as a natural part of our lives.

War will not truly be ended by the obsolete machinations of muddled mystics thrusting their preconceptions and misconceptions on a population they hold in contempt. And overwhelming force will not end war.

War will only be ended by a general enlightenment – all over the world – nothing fancy, just enough awareness to allow us to reach the level of any slightly civilized planet.

And EVP has a part to play in enabling that.

There is no guarantee that we will be wanted. Like the men at "Deep Seven", we may be banned, barred or evicted.

But if we do what we can, our chances may be better. It would be quite a good idea to leave all flags, politics, ideas of rights and constitutions, favored nations and chosen people back in the old physical universe – the rules up-top could be rather different – and remember the camel who tried to get through the eye of the needle. Leave the baggage behind.

Unless you become as little children – children are untroubled by the sort of baggage we lug around. At least, that is the way it used to be. Now – it is a harsh and competitive world, the US has become like one vast car-boot sale populated by people with four elbows and forked tongues.

We have a lot to learn about I-space – and that is one of the joys of this activity – the joy of discovery – and of playing a part in evolution.

A Look at the Future

If we can keep on pushing on through on EVP, reaching more and more people, funding ourselves through our own efforts so that we can pay people to take this up as their profession – we will have taken Mankind a hundred, two hundred, three hundred years ahead.

Take a look at what the futurists are predicting – oh, smarter computers, Hologram TV – another of the research areas in which patents have been applied for – all these sort of easily predictable cutesy little developments.

I tell you – if you want a laugh – watch some of those old future-forecasting TV programs – they nearly always get it wrong.

Even people like the European governments get it wrong. In a sensible move they decided to make funds available for possible future developments. Which is fine – but the people they select to decide on what is going to be the thing of the future are academics – teachers – a worthy profession but not ideas people. And so you get vast sums of development money being poured into plans that in some cases are obsolete before they begin.

Don't let them tell you what the future is going to be. They have a track record of getting it wrong.

One of the things in recent times in the UK was Call-Centers – all the depressed areas with old industries – coal, steel, shipbuilding – were to switch over to the new sunrise industries – Call-Centers.

So young people joined in droves for what were really sweatshop jobs. And now the Call-Centers are closing and going overseas to cheaper countries. What a wonderful bit of foresight that was.

Properly resourced and organized there is no real reason why in the next 10 years or so, EVP should not be as common as, and as clear as – say – the early telephones were.

What this means – and this is the important point – this is the most important point – everyone exposed to EVP will have an experience of and an appreciation of the informational universe – the spiritual universe.

And that is going to set a lot of new perspectives. Perspectives that will incline to more understanding of the Big Scene and why so much conflict is wasteful, barbaric and unnecessary.

Chapter Fourteen

Space, Time, and Information

I have been suggesting the concept of Information as a form
of "space" – Information Space – I-space – since 1976 – when
we called it P-space, probability space, but it was 1989 before I
released the first documents about I-space as a new dimension.

As time passes we welcome others to this point of view –
whether they have got there by their own unaided efforts or
with our help.

One such person is Professor Arie Issar, Emeritus Professor of
the Hebrew University of Jerusalem.

Robert L. Constable of Cornell University in his notes on the
'What is Information' conference, writes,

> 'Over the course of four and a half days, forty
> scientists from four countries considered the question,
> "What is information?"
>
> ...
>
> Surrounded by the stark beauty of the desert setting
> for the Workshop, at Sde Boker in the Negev, the
> participants were drawn together in common
> realization of the special opportunity at hand.'

And he concludes with,

> 'Professor Issar's wish to express within only one set
> of coordinates the evolution of the form of
> hominids.... and the evolution of their intelligence....
> brought him to the suggestion to add to space-time an
> additional dimension, which he defined as
> "information."

OK – we are not going to get involved here with the evolution
of hominids (man-like creatures such as apes and forms of
early man), but the rest is more or less what is being suggested
here.

No one has really looked at Information as a dimension before – but it is essential for our understanding of EVP and how it comes about, to do so.

And that is why we call Information the New Dimension – it is actually a whole lot of dimensions wrapped up in one. A bit like Einstein's Space-Time diagram, as shown in Figure 1.

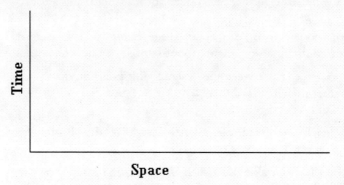

Space

Figure 1

The three dimensions of space are just shown as one dimension – all three are wrapped up as one dimension – in this diagram. And that is all it is – just a diagram. If you have a problem with this don't blame me – this is Einstein's diagram!

For example on the diagram you could show the life of someone – say Maria Correlli. Born in Rome in 1916, died in New York in 1990 – locations in space and in time.

When we add the Information Dimension, see the Figure below, we get a three-dimensional diagram with Information as the third dimension. (Of course, Space actually has three dimensions, and with Time the fourth, that makes Information the fifth dimension.)

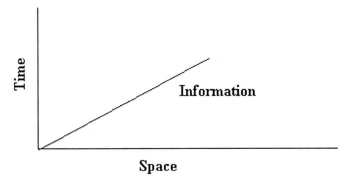

Space

Figure 2

Now this becomes quite interesting – quite interesting to a person with a scientific mind – everyone else, stick with it, its not so bad!

The thing is you can't see Time. What we see is <u>change</u> – the hands on the clock going around, the figures on the calendar changing – all these things we can see – and we say that this is caused by Time.

Information we can observe, time we cannot. All we know about time is through information, or more exactly, <u>change in information</u> – the position of the clock hands, the figures shown on the display.

So what we are really seeing is change of information – and we can show that on the diagram as a slope and the slope corresponds to the velocity of light. (Just thought you'd want to know that)!

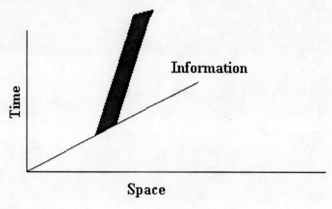

Figure 3

The rate of change of information is the rate at which today becomes the past and the future becomes today.

So – physical universe information is like a sheet of information at an angle to time.

That slice of information represents the physical universe as we know it.

Now just as we can't see time – but we can see *change*; so also we can't see space – but what we can see *separation*. Space, like Time, is invisible.

What this means is that the "space" that we can see is the *separateness* of things, and this skews the "space" that we see, as in Figure 4 below.

This is the way that advanced cosmologists refer to our universe, now – as a membrane – or 'brane – much like a slice of bread in a loaf.

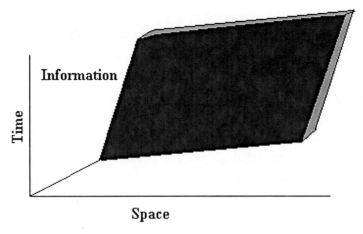

Figure 4

And just as the slope of information against time was a velocity – the rate of flow of change, so too, the slope of information against space is "spaciousness."

The spaciousness of space in the physical universe is fixed. Just as it is a constant, c, the speed of light, that fixes the rate of flow of information; so it is another constant, pi, that fixes the spaciousness of space.

Try this. Hold out your arm out in front of you, straight from the shoulder, and clench the fist.

Now look at your knuckles far away there in the distance and keep looking at them, and imagine that they are 10 feet away.

Then, stop doing that, and imagine instead that your knuckles are just two inches away.

That was all in the mind – and it was just to give an idea of what spaciousness means.

They tell you the universe is 'expanding'.

Has this ever struck you as a little strange?

Here you have the universe, which includes all of time and all of space – and yet it is expanding – which means it is moving into yet another space outside itself ... except, there is no space outside itself– it is the totality of space itself.

What they really mean when they say, 'the universe is expanding' is that the universe is getting more spacious. As an illustration of "getting more spacious" – instead of your knuckles looking like 2 inches away they are now looking like 10 feet away.

The reason that it is mentioned here is that spaciousness can be a noticeable feature of I-space. In a good presence there will tend to be a great sense of spaciousness and light, in a bad presence there will be a sense of compression and darkness.

These things follow with a similar logic to that of normal physics and mathematics.

Spiritual Force

There is also an informational version of 'force' – informational force, (spiritual force, sometimes also referred to as psychic force).

The attractive force is Liking. (This word is used rather than 'love' as love gets confused with sex and relationships and gender and emotions).

Liking is force – the rest are side-effects and reactions to it, and reactions to the reactions, and judgments about reactions. In itself it is purely a force. The force of attraction.

The liking can be general, an overall 'sunniness', low power, though the person may seem to have a certain presence.

Or it can be focussed and intensely powerful; in which case the force may be quite evident.

The other force – the pushing away force – is dislike. (This word is used rather than 'hate' as that also has a lot of emotional baggage with it involving emotions and violence, and reactions, and reactions to reactions, and judgments about reactions.)

It too can be quite mild – a generalized gloominess, low powered; though the person may seem to want to be absent.

We are just touching on these things here so that we can consider why EVP has to be at all, and how come there are different informational beings. All the bits and pieces you are getting will add up to the final explanation.

Before we leave Liking and Disliking there is one related phenomenon that we have to consider – Reverse Action.

Reverse Action

The primary action of Liking is to get closer to; the primary action of Disliking is to get further away from.

One would suppose that a person who had a great liking for a lot of things would end up with all those things close, and a person who had a great dislike for a lot of things would end up with all those things driven far away.

But a reverse action is what happens. The person with great liking "expands out" to be with the things that are so greatly liked. They are more "spacious" – it is good to be in their space.

The person who has a great disliking compresses in to get away from their dislikes, and in so doing, they bring them in and become the victim of their dislikes. In their presence one feels closed in and an urge to get away.

The environment that people live in can have a great effect on their outlook and prospects – but it is never the last word.

The Nature of Dimensions

The phenomenon of dimensions also holds for the Informational Universe, and has two properties that will be familiar to those with a scientific background.

These can be described as Quantity and Quality – or scale and nature.

Scale

If one is on a scan in I-space – if one is "traveling" in the Informational Universe, then what happens along a dimension line is that the scale gets bigger.

If you keep the nature of the experience the same – say, mountains and snow, then the "further" you go the higher the mountains and the deeper the snow. That is going in an "Outward" or advancing direction. Going in an "Inward" or retreating direction the scale gets smaller.

But as well as going "Outward" or "Inward" you can also Diverge – you can turn "Left" or "Right" – and remember information has many dimensions, so you could turn not just "Left", but (I will make-up some names) you could turn Laft, or Loft, or Lift, or Luft, or Raght or Roght or Reght or Rught or.... You get the idea?

Quality

If you *Diverge*, then it is not the *scale* that alters it is the *Quality* or nature of the experience. So, if the experience is that of mountains and snow, and you Diverge, then the experience is not of larger or smaller mountains and snow, it is of a change of quality. The nature of the experience changes. So you might find that you have changed from mountains and snow to a forest and a stream, or curl around some more and you could come on a desert and palm trees, and curl around some more and you could come on a wild sea and hurricanes.

Yes – you find all these in the physical universe also – but they are not all arranged according to similarity – they occur where they occur in accordance with physical laws.

In the Informational Universe – in I-space – if you Diverge (Div.) you change the quality of the experience – its nature changes.

That is fine – but if you turn too sharply, if the Div. value is too high, then you may experience a "surprise" as a reaction to the changed nature of the experience. (As the Amsterdam tourist people used to put it, 'Around every corner a little surprise' and show a picture of a canal. And as the Dutch humorist put it, 'Around every corner a little surprise,' and showed around the corner a little pile of doggie do-dos – such was the state of Amsterdam's streets).

An even higher Div. value or a rapid Curl – which is just a continuing divergence – can lead to experiencing shock – which is where all this is leading to.

So – magnify surprise and it becomes shock.

Just as the further Outward the traverse, the greater the scale, so in Divergence the sharper the curvature, the greater the change in quality.

It is a natural event. No Kings and no Lords, no territories and no enemies.

Emotions, Reactions and Energy

In terms of scale what induces emotion is relative scale. The Grand Canyon induces *awe* in millions; it is a World Heritage Site. The significant factor is scale. If the Grand Canyon were the size of a small ditch it would induce no awe, no one would come to see it. It would probably get filled in. It is a matter of relative scale.

Or looking at it the other way, if one were on the same scale as the Grand Canyon one would not be awed by it. One might keep it as a garden feature – on the other hand one might want a pool there, the Colorado stream being handy, and it wouldn't need much digging up. It is a matter of relative scale.

The onset of liking has side-effects – and the faster the onset the greater the strength of the side-effects. The side-effects are the various positive emotions.

The onset of disliking has side-effects – and the faster the onset the greater the strength of the side-effects. The side-effects are the various negative emotions.

Once liking is established, then a state of tension exists between the liker and the liked, and this is called Desire. This is positive energy.

Once disliking is established, then a state of tension exists between the disliker and the disliked, and this is called Revulsion. This is negative energy.

Both Desire and Revulsion are potentials – once you have got what you want then you may no longer want it; once you have lost what you did not want you might no longer feel revulsion.

In many physical universe situations one communicates one's emotions – with words or body language or in the tone of voice – and that can provoke an emotional; reaction in other person – which they will communicate with words or body language or in the tone of voice – and to which one may react with reinforced emotions or new emotions, and on them base standpoints or attitudes if there is any sort of conflict involved.

In fact it may be true to say that as humans we live in an ever-boiling emotional soup in which we cannot separate our own emotions from those induced in one by others – which in turn we may have induced in these others – and so on.

The Informational being is also capable of duplicating the emotion of another – we would call that Compassion.

The Informational Universe has its own situations.

One may be happily going along and then make a slight Div., when suddenly one is confronted by something one dislikes intensely.

In handling that there are two strategies,

- Retreat, which diminishes one's scale, (is compressive),

- Turn away from, which might work, or it may lead into the path of something even worse. That in turn leads to a still more rapid retreat and a still sharper divergence.

If the situation is not resolved through these actions, what can result is a rapid curling and retreat – a simultaneous spiraling and scale reduction – in other words a contracting spinning-in – a compressive spiral. The displaced energy resulting from this compression seems to go into a "downward component" – so that the compressive spiral becomes a contracting vortex.

This is the basis of an I-space black hole.

The Vortex

> 'And it came to pass, when the Lord would take Elijah up into Heaven by a whirlwind, that Elijah went with Elisha from Gilgal.'
>
> II. Kings, 2. 1

Expanding on the theory of the Black Hole in Information Space, and using black holes in physical space as an analogy, the process would be as follows.

Information would be "drawn into" the Black Hole. And note that this refers to Information Space, not the physical universe – where the theory of black holes seems to have been thrown into confusion by recent statements about information and black holes by the Professor of Mathematics at Cambridge, Stephen Hawking. I will expand on this a little in case anyone reading of it might consider it to be the same as I-space black hole theory.

In July 2004, Professor Hawking corrected his previous black hole theory to agree that information cannot be destroyed. Hawking had led the field in our understanding of black holes -- matter-consuming vortices created when stars collapse.

Under the banner headline,

'Hawking unveils new thinking on black holes

Famed physicist says vortexes do not destroy all they consume'

MSNBC News[33] carries an Associated Press article saying,

> 'In 1997, [Hawking, Professor of Mathematics at Cambridge] and Caltech physics professor Kip Thorne made a well-publicized bet with a particle physicist, John Preskill, that "information swallowed by a black hole is forever hidden from the outside universe and can never be revealed, even as the black hole evaporates and completely disappears.
>
> Preskill, also a Caltech professor, insisted that information on a black hole's consumption "must and will be found in the correct theory of quantum gravity."'

Present thinking on black holes in the physical universe is slightly confused, but does not affect our thinking on the giant black hole in I-space which led to "The Fall."

---

[33] http://www.msnbc.msn.com/id/5473323/

With regard to Information Space, the black hole "draws in" Information. This is the same as loss of spaciousness would be in physical space. The corresponding thing to spaciousness in physical space, is potentiality in I-space, in other words, unlimited possibilities.

So as I-space is "drawn in" there is a loss of possibilities. With less possibilities there is thus a growth of probability, and a loss of information. The less the possibilities the stronger probability becomes.

There is less freedom. There is an increase in determinism in "enforcement." As I-space gets drawn in, it "condenses" into *probabilities* which in turn determine *patterns*. These are the ancestors of physical laws. When in Yoga, Theosophy, and other teachings, they speak of *denser* planes this is what they are referring to. We are simply putting it in modern language.

As well as being drawn in, there is a spiraling, and so *cyclic* patterning is imposed on Information.

As mentioned previously the being has its location in I-space determined by its thoughts – the information it is focussed on, and so as the Information gets drawn in, the being "follows" it, wanting to resist losing it.

Beings are pulled in as they try to resist their losses, and undergoing a massive spinning compression, effectively "die."

The emotion emanating from dying beings results in more and more being drawn in through the force of Compassion – which further energizes the system.

Spun-in beings are then re-born in loss and deprivation, compressed and spinning with time.

Welcome to the Physical Universe.

The Lost Paradise, Home – gone.

But ... a nagging little question remains....

Chapter Fifteen

The Fall and its Consequences

There is one other little question. This same scenario could happen without anything happening to I-space. The whole cycle of activity could simply be due to the being itself, spinning and compressing, all in its own "mind." This makes more sense than imagining that all of I-space changed. Here, the "Original Sin" is in the mind of the "fallen" being that finds itself here on earth.

But, if anything deserved the name the Fall this was it. And, coincidentally, if there had been no Good-Bad knowledge the whole thing might never have happened. This version is, if anything, closer to the Qur'ân, in that one is responsible for one's own fall.

Where the original of the story the Hebrews related in the Bible came from is not known. A Shamanic origin has been suggested, as it is completely different from the Babylonian story of the falling into disrepute of Adapa, who was *already* on Earth The Babylonian story was once suggested as the source of the Hebrew Fall story.

Another possibility worth mentioning is that the Black Hole phenomenon could perhaps lead to an *informational* being appearing or having some presence in the physical Universe – without a body. What I am suggesting here is that this could explain the presence of discarnates and many of the voices in EVP sessions.

As a new idea this should be examined more closely but it could also be an explanation for why a significant percentage of the voices are in distress – are, in fact, spun-in and depressed.

Looking at the Black Hole phenomenon from another perspective, we know from such writers as Robert Monroe that a white hole in the distance is the point to aim for in the early stages of Out of the Body Experiences. The technique being to advance towards this light and then to withdraw from it, and to do this over and over again, to build up confidence.

One of the former prisoners in Alcatraz, the prison in San Francisco Bay, would be put in solitary confinement now and then. Alone and in total darkness he was still able to escape.

He noticed ahead of him what appeared to be a spot of white light. By "moving" out and through that light he was able to travel wherever he wanted.

'Iron bars do not a prison make'.

The rule also seems to be – white hole means ascendance, black hole means descent.

The master of the Out of Body Experience (OOBE), the late Robert Monroe, in his first OOBEs, spun out of the body with a rotational movement.

In his books he deals with the fascinating things that he finds during his OOBEs, but if you go right back to the beginning, when he first started, just after his first few "accidental" experiences, what did he actually do? What was the process involved?

Here, in his own words, is a quote from his first book, 'Journeys Out of The Body'.

> '9/10/58 Afternoon

> Again, I floated upward, with the intent of visiting Dr Bradshaw and his wife.

> Again came the turning in air, the dive into the tunnel, and this time the sensation of going uphill....'

Note the turning in the air – what we would call 'spin', the mention of the word 'tunnel' and a sensation of going 'up'. When we come to discuss Near Death Experiences this may be more meaningful, but for the moment note that we have a spin allied to a progressive motion - in other words a vortex.

What we are dealing with are vortices.

Until Einstein came along with his Theory of Relativity, and sparked off Quantum Theory at the beginning of the last Century, the theory of Vortices was considered by many scientists to have the greatest potential for explaining the fundamentals of the physical universe.

The following is said of Lord Kelvin, past President of the Royal Society, and buried in Westminster Abbey next to Sir Isaac Newton,

> 'It was his theory of the atom in terms of vortices that attracted wide attention.

> In fact for a time the theory of vortices was considered to be capable of answering all the questions that the scientists of that day had about atomic theory.'

There is another way we can get to the spin factor. So far we have started at the "top" – the informational universe and worked our way down. Now we are going to start with the physical universe at its most basic and work our way up.

The figure below shows a straight line – you could imagine it as a pencil, but so slim that we could consider it one-dimensional – that is, having length but no thickness.

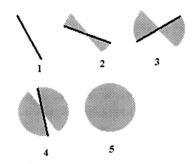

Now imagine spinning that line – and the shape it will trace out is a disc.

That is a 2-dimensional figure.

Spin a 1 dimensional line and you get a 2 dimensional disc.

Rotating a line traces out a disc

In the figure above a line is rotated from position 1 through to 2, 3, 4, and on to position 5. In being spun, thus, in being rotated, the shape it traces out is a disc – a two-dimensional shape.

Spin a line – one-dimension – and you get a disc – two dimensions. The rotation produces a dimensional step-up transformation.

In spinning the line what we have made it do is to take up every position available to it within its own bounds – its own one-dimensional "universe". Its been through it all.

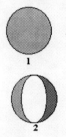

Now lets push this on another step. Next, spin the 2-dimensional disc, 1, through stages 2 and 3 and on – and what you get is a sphere – a 3-dimensional space.

2-D spun, gives 3-D

Spin a 2 dimensional space and you get a 3-dimensional space.

1-D spun gives a 2-D space, a 2-D space, spun, gives a 3-D space.

The Spinning Sphere

Will a 3-D space, spun, give us a 4-dimensional space?

Now imagine spinning the sphere.

And what do you get?

You get a spinning sphere.

And that is the 4th dimension. Time, as evidenced by change, is now a factor. Spin a 3 dimensional space and you get a 4-dimensional space – you get 3-space with spin. The 4th dimension is commonly recognized as time – which ties in quite well with what we have been saying.

The spinning is a flow of change – which we take as being time.

You even get a close analogy in all this.

It is almost as though God was saying – "Look, kids, now this is how it works – watch the pretty planet...."

The pretty planet spins and what do you get – day turning from dim dawn to bright morning; the bright morning turning into the even brighter afternoon; and then fading away to the

---

184

darkness of the night. That is the spinning of the planet Earth – and that is what we call a day – 24 hours – and 24 hours is of course an amount of time.

And what creates these 24 hours – this standard amount of time?

Why – the planet spinning on its axis of course. The spinning sphere.

Now what we are interested in, here, is not planet earth spinning on its axis – what we are interested in is the spin of all space, we are saying that space has an intrinsic spin – it has a built-in spin.

And because we are **in** space, we cannot see the spin. If you walk down the corridor of a train traveling at 70 mph you dont see the train hurtling towards you at 70 mph – that is because you are also traveling at 70 mph.

So, in the case of spinning space, we are also traveling with the spin, and so are unaware of it. Just as we are unaware of the fact that – right now – on this planet, we are spinning around at round a thousand miles per hour. You and I are spinning around at nearly 1000 miles an hour.

Space itself is spinning. But we don't know it.

There is nothing *outside* space, so we can't see that we are spinning. There is nothing to give us a reference. Traveling on the train at 70mph all you have to do is look out the window to see that you are hurtling along at 70mph. But with space there is no "window", and even if there was a window there would be nothing to see – because there is no "outside" – there is only "inside." All that the universe contains is "inside". And by definition a universe is the totality of what it contains.

So with the spin there is nothing to see outside to check that we are spinning.

Well ... that's not quite true. There is one way. There is a factor that shows that the spin exists and how fast it is.

Seeing the Spin

You have heard about what Einstein called the Space-Time continuum. What he said, quite rightly, was that if you travel in space you also travel in time.

For example, if I walk from *Here* the 10 yards to *There*, then I have traveled in space. And let us say that it took me *two seconds* to travel that distance. Then the point that we are calling *There* is two seconds into the future from when I first set out. I traveled 10 yards in space and 2 seconds into the future in making this journey. Space and time are part of the same thing, said Einstein. You cannot travel in space without traveling in time too. I traveled 10 yards and 2 seconds. The point we called *There* that I arrived at was *10 yards away* in space and *two seconds* away in time.

Einstein felt that he had to use a new word to describe that complicated something composed partly of space and partly of time – and the word he chose was "*continuum*" – meaning that space and time were linked together as components of this thing – this "continuum".

So what he was saying, in effect, was that space and time were dimensions of the continuum – space contributing three dimensions and time contributing one – the 4th dimension.

But have you wondered why with space you can go any way you want – outward, inward, sideways, up and down, forward and backward – but in time you can only go one way – forward – into the future.

Ooooh big problem, big problem – what is going on here – help!

Space and time are supposed to be equivalent but in time you can only go one way – into the future.

Why?

The River of Time

Well, sit ye down by the fire and I will tell you what folk do say, like.

They do say that time is a river – ever flowing, bringing us new tomorrows and taking away old yesterdays – the River of Time.

That's what they do say in them there Universities. An' they ought to know – what with all them books and all....

Well, my friend if you do say that what they do say is *wrong* – or even, if you do say that what they do say is a load of old *crap* – then let me shake your hand – put it there, pardner.

I mean – where is all this unused time coming from? Is there some great reservoir of **Unused Time** out there, upstream ahead of us, where all our Tomorrows come from?

And is there some great reservoir of **Used Time** downstream of us, where all our Yesterdays go to?

The idea of time "flowing" is a bit silly, really – where is it flowing from, exactly?

And, indeed, where is it flowing to?

If it is flowing then it must be coming from somewhere and going to somewhere else - that is in the very definition of flowing.

It is another case of easily accepted concepts that nobody questions. But science is about questioning.

I once had a student who was always questioning everything. He was a darned nuisance and I had thought of holding him up to ridicule on every possible occasion, slowly "destroying" him – or at least that rebellious spirit, making him conform for the good of the group – the way that "teachers" can do – but I also saw that I would have destroyed life – vitality.

Maybe that is what society would want – but I saw in there a kindred spirit – and I let the questions continue.

He never became a great scientist – but he became outstanding in his chosen field.

So, let the questioning continue.

You cannot have a flow without implying a "where from" and also a "where to." It stands to reason, if you have a flow it must be coming from somewhere and going to somewhere else. So where is the flow coming from and where is it going to?

In truth, fashionable belief though it may be – there are no reservoirs; there is no River Of Time.

This is a daft idea which has been around for thousands of years and which is still treated as though it was common-sense among many people who haven't actually considered how absurd the whole idea is.

Just as this planet, Earth, is spinning at a speed of about 1000 miles per hour right at this moment and we are unaware of it, so the space that we occupy is spinning at (roughly) 186,000 miles per second – the speed of light – and we are unaware of that also. It is the rate at which the present becomes the past and the future becomes the present. It is the rate of spin.

And it is this spin that is carrying us remorselessly on into the future.

You get the idea? The reason we can't go back into the past is because *we are being carried forward into the future by this universal spin.*

That is the main point I was going to make.

The Hierarchy of Dimensions

But there are two other points that come out of this.

1.   Note that there is a hierarchy of dimensions.

Three dimensional space contains two-dimensional space, and two dimensional space contains one-dimensional space. And talking of the space-time continuum, 4-dimensional space contains 3-dimensional space.

And, as it is all information, we can say that 5-dimensional space contains 4-dimensional space. Also, as you go up in number of dimensions you go up in universal energy – a three-dimensional universe would have more energy potential than a two-dimensional space and a two-dimensional space more energy potential than a one-dimensional.

And if we go up from a four-dimensional physical universe to a 5-dimensional universe – which contains the 4-dimenions as a component – then we go up another energy step.

Now, here is something to be aware of. All we know about the physical universe is all we *know* about it.

If we didn't know anything about it – then, so far as we would be concerned, it would not exist.

All we know about the universe is what we know about it. And what we know about it is information – everything we know about the physical universe is *information*.

But that sector of information is not the *totality* of information – it is just a part of the totality of information.

And this is what we mean when we say that the physical universe is a sub-set of the informational universe.

So we have gone here from purely physical considerations to a higher level of universe, and we have involved the concept of spin. And what we are talking about is the linking of one universe to another.

The Chinese have a legend that this was the state of affairs in pre-historical times, with traffic going both up and down – but at some time before recorded history this ceased.

And from the Bible the Hebrew, Jacob, had a dream.

> 'And he dreamed that there was a ladder set up on the earth, and the top of it reached to heaven; and behold, the angels of God were ascending and descending on it.'

This is the dream that Jacob had one night when he slept in the desert with stones for a pillow. (Genesis 28, 12.)

The pagan Celts had a rather casual attitude to passing from one realm to the next, according to Professor Nora Chadwick,[34]

---

[34] Page 181 'The Celts', by Professor Nora Chadwick, Penguin Books (1991).

'I would call attention to the naturalness with which men, women and the gods meet and pass in and out of the natural and the supernatural spheres.'

This all ties in quite well with Yogi philosophy.

And there is another feature that should be noted.

I have mentioned planetary spin – 24 hours per rotation – and I have mentioned universal spin – but have not tried to indicate a cycle time for that.

Physical science is not at present able to suggest a figure because although beliefs from the Native South Americans to the Hindi have spoken of cycles of time, our philosophers have been dedicated to the "wonderfully logical", award-winning *River of Time* principle.

2.   If you look into the Yogic philosophy in more detail – and Yogic Philosophy is not all about standing on your head for two hours – then you will find that they speak of time as being in Kalpas – giant spirals or vortices of a cyclic nature.

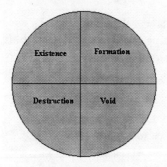

It is said that a Kalpa is represented by a period of four hundred and thirty two million years. The four Kalpas of a) Formation, b) Existence, c) Destruction and d) Emptiness, as a complete cycle is called a Maha Kalpa or Great Kalpa.

I have replaced the word

Great Kalpa Cycle

emptiness with the word Void to relate it to Western teachings. In fact all the words could do with a tidy-up but that is not our purpose here – and anyway the words that we have are words that have undergone translation into English.

And we can refer to more modern sources. David Ash B.Sc. and Peter Hewitt M.A. (Cantab.) in their book, "Vortices", [35] make a statement almost identical to my own.

Note that they have never read my material and until very recently I had read none of theirs.

What they say is,

> '[Einstein] saw time and space as being inextricably linked, with time as a fourth dimension.
>
> Is there some fundamental process in the universe on which all other measures of time could be built? Spin in the vortex could well be this ultimate process.
>
> This account of space and time casts new light on Relativity. For example, curved space and time is fundamental to Relativity. The vortex picture shows very clearly how space-time can be curved....
>
> If the speed of movement in the vortex is the speed of light, then it is obvious why space, time and matter are all linked, and related to the speed of light.'

Which is exactly what we have been saying here.

It is nice to have confirmation, but now lets see if one of the world's foremost cosmologists has something to say which might interest us.

Million-dollar prize-winning physicist Professor Paul Davies, in addressing the subject of 'The ultimate origin of the universe,' in his book "The Cosmic Blueprint," writes as follows.

> '[Another Theory] holds that time in some sense 'turns into' space near the origin, so that rather than considering the appearance of three-dimensional space at an instant of time, one instead deals with a four–dimensional space. If this space is taken to curve around smoothly to form an unbroken continuum, there is then no real origin at all.'

---

[35] Page 61, 'The Vortex', Ash and Hewitt, Gateway Books, bath.

Professor Davies is not describing a vortex here, but as you can see, if you are willing to consider 4-dimensional space that does not mean you are some kind of weirdo – nor does a related interest in religion - it was for that he received the million dollar Templeton prize.

Davies is one of the top minds of this time as can be seen from the biographical details on his webpage.

> [As well as his interest in} physics, Davies is also interested in the nature of time, high-energy particle physics, the foundations of quantum mechanics, the origin of life and the nature of consciousness.

> [He] was awarded the 2001 Kelvin Medal by the UK Institute of Physics, and the 2002 Michael Faraday Prize by the Royal Society, the 1995 Templeton Prize for progress in religion, the world's largest prize for intellectual endeavour, presented by Prince Philip at Buckingham Palace. The prize ceremony, held at Westminster Abbey, was attended by 700 people'.

This is not to suggest that Davies knows anything about EVP

or would agree with what we are doing - what I am trying to get across is the idea that first class thinkers tend to be bold and are a complete contrast to our critics.

Note the names above – Kelvin, Faraday and the Royal Society.

There have been a number of other big names involved with the

William Thomson, Lord Kelvin

concept of the vortex as it applied to physics and the fundamentals of the universe.

Two of these are mentioned in Ash and Hewitt's book, "Vortex", referred to above.

These are two of the biggest names one could find in the history of science.

One is J.J. Thomson, Belfast born Scot, a professor at only 22, he later was to become Lord Kelvin, President of the Royal Society, the foremost scientific institution in the UK. He was awarded the Order of Merit and was buried in Westminster Abbey next to Sir Isaac Newton. The first scientist ever to be buried in the Abbey - a singular honor.

He was a founding father of thermodynamics and the Kelvin scale of temperature is named after him.

In his time very little was known about the atom but it was his theory of the atom in terms of vortices that attracted wide attention.

In fact for a time the theory of vortices was considered to be capable of answering all the questions that the scientists of that day had about atomic theory.

James Clerk Maxwell - whose names lives on in Maxwell's Equations - wrote,

> '... the vortex ring ... imagined as the true form of the atom by Thomson, satisfies more of the conditions than any atom hitherto imagined.'

As Ash and Hewitt put it in their book,

> 'Maxwell was a major advocate of the vortex. He was convinced it was the best explanation for matter that had ever been put forward.'

We are here speaking of the giants of physics. Clerk Maxwell became the first professor of experimental physics at the University of Cambridge and founded the world famous Cavendish Laboratory there.

James Clerk Maxwell

Richard Feynman, a major figure in Quantum Mechanics, and a Nobel Laureate said,

'From a long view of ... history ... there can be little doubt that the most significant event of the 19th century will be judged as Maxwell's discovery of the laws of electrodynamics.'

When we are talking blithely about vortices, we ought to be aware of the caliber of those who went before.

But there is yet another giant on our side - his name was also Thomson. J.J Thomson - and he too was knighted, to become Sir J.J. Thomson. And he too became President of the Royal Society, and in his turn he too was buried among the Truly Great in Westminster Abbey. He too was head of the Cavendish Laboratory.

Thomson was of course the discoverer of the electron - the fundamental particle that is the whole and entire basis of electronics. But even in his early days he had shown a great interest in the properties of the vortex, I quote,

'Thomson's early interest in atomic structure was reflected in his *Treatise on the Motion of Vortex Rings* which won him the Adams Prize in 1884. In 1892 he had his *Notes on Recent Researches in Electricity and Magnetism* published. This is often referred to as "the third volume of Maxwell"*.

Here, and again I quote Ash and Hewitt, is some of what he had to say about vortices,

Sir J.J. Thomson

'[The vortex atom] has very strong [theory-based]recommendations in its favor ... the vortex theory of matter is of a much more fundamental character than the ordinary solid particle theory.'

These people were virtually creating the future - the 20th and even the 21st Century.

To add to the "team" – here is another who helped make the world the way it is – and while it would be mere name-dropping to count Kelvin, Clerk Maxwell and Thomson as in any way connected with EVP, here is one giant who did practice EVP.

His name was Alec Reeves. Alec was the inventor of Pulse Code Modulation, PCM, without which there would be no cellular phones or Internet. This guy, who invented PCM and who was also involved in early research into fiber optic cables, (without which we would have no cable TV and would probably still have expensive phone calls), this giant of electronics was also researching EVP.

Reeves was also ahead of the para game in another respect also. He had devised a method whereby a random particle flow – in the experiments, ball bearings – could show a tendency to favor either right or left. And by assessing which was the greater – right or left – interpretations in a Yes/No form could be made.

In actual fact this sort of technique – now using atomic particles – is used by the Princeton Engineering Anomalies Research people in their PK experiments. And you can find such methods used as a test of PK on the Net. But do you think there is any acknowledgment of the work of Alec Harley Reeves?

He had a couple of lesser lights associated with him. David Ellis - who you know about - who researched EVP while he was doing an MA degree at Cambridge, and his technical advisor, a fellow-student who was doing a Bachelor's degree in Electronics, John de Rivaz.

John is a terribly caring person who is now the head of the cryogenics movement (freezing a dead person's brain) in the UK. But way back in his student days, John, worried about the effect that Mr. Reeves' interest in EVP could be having on his mental health, became rather against EVP and thus also did his friend David Ellis.

But to be fair, we must say that none of that had anything much to do with Cambridge – and nothing at all to do with the Cavendish.

Now at the Cavendish is Nobel Laureate Brian Josephson whose work is involved with theories linking Mind and Matter.

He has a web-page devoted to the paranormal. If I may quote from his website

'Welcome to the home page of Professor

Brian Josephson

> Brian Josephson, director of the Mind-Matter Unification Project of the Theory of Condensed Matter Group at the Cavendish Laboratory, Cambridge, a project concerned primarily with the attempt to understand, from the viewpoint of the theoretical physicist, what may loosely be characterised as intelligent processes in nature associated with brain function or with some other natural process.'

So - let us hear no more about scientific conspiracies. It is not scientists who have held up the progress of EVP. You will note the prominence of Cambridge and the Cavendish Laboratory in all this – and of course the Royal Society.

And who precisely are the opposition? Fifth-raters whose only claim to fame and thus media attention is that they want to stop EVP. How sad.

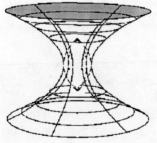

OK – now lets get back to get back to inter-dimensional communications.

Here is a drawing showing a black hole connected to a white

Black hole – White Hole   hole via what is called a "wormhole." But what is interesting here is simply the vortex shapes, above and below.

The picture below shows a black hole leading to a white hole – from a different angle. We might think of it as showing the edges of the vortex connecting an upper universe to a lower one – or a lower universe connecting to an upper one.

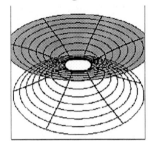

Black hole/White hole, another view

I would like to quote from Website, http://casa.colorado.edu/~ajsh/home.html.

This is the website of Andrew Hamilton, Professor at the Department of Astrophysical and Planetary Sciences, University of Colorado at Boulder, an expert on black holes, white holes, and wormholes.

The presence of a quote here is not meant to imply that Professor Hamilton approves or has even heard of EVP.

What I am hoping to show here is the presence of parallel concepts.

What Professor Hamilton says, is,

> 'The complete Schwarzschild[36] geometry consists of a black hole, a white hole, and two Universes connected at their horizons by a wormhole. . A white hole is a black hole running backwards in time. Just as black holes swallow things irretrievably, so also do white holes spit them out. White holes cannot exist, since they violate the second law of thermodynamics.

---

[36] Schwarzschild was a German mathematician who died in 1916 who had done some very important work in Relativity and other subjects.

General Relativity is time symmetric. It does not know about the second law of thermodynamics, and it does not know about which way cause and effect go. But we do.

The negative square root solution outside the horizon represents another Universe. The wormhole joining the two separate Universes is known as the Einstein-Rosen bridge.'[37]

What he says is that a white-hole is actually a black-hole running backwards in time.

It sounds complicated – but it is actually *very* relevant to EVP.

Look at it this way.

The Video Tape Example

Suppose you were watching a video of a black hole – you would see all the stuff – stars and planets and what looks like luminous dust – swirling along in circles spiraling closer and closer to the middle of the vortex – being sucked in and being sucked down – disappearing from sight, <u>going in to</u> the Black Hole.

That is the black hole scene.

OK – sticking with this illustration of watching a video tape – now make it slowly *rewind* – and what do you see? You see it all running in reverse – 'backwards in time' as Professor Hamilton states it.

You would see the stuff – stars and planets and what looks like luminous dust – appearing <u>to come out of</u> the black hole, being hurled out in a spiral of ever-widening circles – just as what we imagine a *white*-hole would do.

And that is terribly significant, and very relevant to the study of EVP.

---

[37] The Einstein-Rosen Bridge is a feature of a black hole, which means that on the other side of the black hole there is another set of dimensions connected in some way with the set from our universe.

Before we relate this concept of 'backwards in time' to EVP, just listen to this account of a Near Death Experience, (NDE).

> 'He traveled through a tunnel and felt that he was traveling back in time.'

And here is another NDE report from that same source,

> 'I was spinning sideways somehow through this tunnel. At first it was very dark, then it seemed like there was these streaks. I was falling but I wasn't. I was traveling. That's maybe more the word. There was this big white light at the end of it. I kind of came out into this.'

This time the word to note is spinning. So we have spin and we have time running backwards. Interesting?

In scientific analysis as in detective work what we are looking for are common factors. EVP looks just like a random event until you note the common factor – all the utterances are short – and when you notice that then you start to make sense of it.

Here we have a physicist talking about *wormholes* and we have people who have experienced NDEs talking about *tunnels* – could it be they are talking about the same thing? Lets look a little further.

The physicist says 'a black hole running backwards in time', the NDE person said, about being in the tunnel, '[That he]felt that he was traveling back in time.'

Co-incidence? I don't think so.

How about the black hole?

Here is another report from Kevin Williams[38] excellent site.

This is definitely the best site on NDEs that I have ever seen. I should point out that all these reports are from different people who had never even heard of each other.

---

[38] www.near-death.com/

> 'Then I began to float upwards and I realized I was having to make a decision. It was almost a physical two-way pull. There seemed to be no ceiling above me, just a black hole into which I was being compelled by a very strong force. It seemed as if I was to make a decision as to which way I would choose to go – up into the tunnel or back into my body.'

Another coincidence – he calls it a black hole. Very interesting.

Then there is the white hole – well, they call it a light at the end of the tunnel – it is an Exit and it goes into white or light, so it meets the white hole definition, even if the exact words are not used. Here are a few excerpts.

> 'I saw a pinpoint of light in the distance. The black mass around me began to take on more of the shape of a tunnel, and I felt myself traveling through it at an even greater speed, rushing toward the light. I was instinctively attracted to it.'

And,

> 'I traveled ... along a tunnel toward a bright light, and I could feel an overwhelming sense of warmth and peace and whiteness. I wanted to walk into the whiteness, which was so tranquil and happy.' (Helen)

Next, three more,

> 'Then I found myself in what appeared to be a large tunnel with a small white light at the other end. I was moving toward this light pretty fast.' (Enigma)

> 'I then remember traveling a long distance upward toward the light. I believe that I was moving very fast, but this entire realm seemed to be outside of time.' (Beverley Brodsky)

> 'I then felt myself moving off very fast, exceedingly fast, into what seemed like outer space. I always felt that it was the fact of going so fast that gave me the sense of being in a tunnel. And I was going toward a very bright light.' (Janet)

OK – there is more, loads more, but all we are doing here is just trying to indicate the common factors between NDE reports and the white hole concept.

Finally, there is another common factor in many, but not all, of the reports – and this has to do with traveling in a wormhole – as physics defines that strange phenomenon.

Quote,

> 'A wormhole is a tunnel in space that matter can traverse through. It works in four dimensions with time being the fourth. It connects two points in the universe.' (Online dictionary).

And,

> 'Einstein first proposed wormholes in 1935. He co-wrote a paper with Nathan Rosen in which they showed that general relativity allowed for what they called "bridges." They theorized that there could be places where space/time is folded that allowed transfer of matter from one point to another in the universe.' (BBC)

But listen to this,

> '... To make things even more fantastic, wormholes could effectively connect not only different parts of the Universe, but even different Universes!'

So – the man says they can even connect different Universes(exclamation point).

Far out.

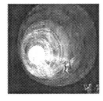

And there we were thinking all along that it was all due to endorphins, or just static and wishful thinking....

One of the main characteristics of wormholes is that they can enable near or beyond light velocities.

The Tunnel as Shown in a Medieval Painting

Almost all the NDE mention the speed of travel through the tunnel. 'I was traveling at the speed of light. As I neared the end of the tunnel, I saw the most brilliant yellow light.' (Beth Hammond)

> '[It]began to take on more of the shape of a tunnel, and I felt myself traveling through it at an even greater speed, rushing toward the light.' (Betty Eadie)

> 'I was flowing. I was flowing toward the light. I was accelerating and I knew I was accelerating, but then again, I didn't really feel the acceleration. I just knew I was accelerating toward the light. Again, the physics was different - the physics of motion of time, space, travel. It was completely different in that tunnel ....' (Barbara Springer)

> 'Simultaneously with the awareness of this tunnel, I had a feeling of forward motion; it was very comfortable, it was very usual. Moving through this tunnel there was an acceleration. There was not any wind vibration, nor any noise. There was no motion sickness or anything like that. It was like floating within a vacuum. I saw that I was increasing speed, but there were no g-forces of the kind you would naturally experience in accelerating movement. I went faster and faster through the tunnel.

> The next empirical knowledge I had was that I had attained at least the speed of light or conceivably faster. Whisking through the tunnel at this speed, I had the depth perception, the visual perception of the tunnel whisking past me *(or I through the tunnel)*.

> The next thing is that way, way off in the distance – to infinity – there appeared this little speck of light. That light was very special; it was the first identifiable object that I was able to focus on, to realize that it was nothing like what I'd seen before. It was extremely bright. This speck of light was brighter than something that would immediately blind you. It was brighter than a million billion carbon arcs, or welder's torches, anything you can possibly compare it to. It was the

brightest thing I'd ever seen in my life'. (Thomas Sawyer)

OK - that will have to do for now. What we have to ask ourselves is why there are so many references to velocity – to speed?

The obvious answer would be that it is a significant feature of what is happening.

So, considering all we have covered – wormholes and tunnels; black holes; white holes and exits into light; noticeably high speeds; connecting Universes – I put it to you that with physicists and NDE people both mentioning the same things – the probability is that they are talking about the same things. There are too many common factors for it just to be a coincidence.

Wormholes in space – where are these wormholes in space?

We are dealing with the Physical Universe and the Informational Universe. Information itself, however, has no physical dimensions. It is not a function of space and it is not a function of time.

Look at it this way. Let us make up a story to illustrate this point.

Suppose we live in a three-dimensional Universe, but there are beings who think that it is only two-dimensional – that it is totally flat.

Then in this 2-D world, at a cocktail party to celebrate the 2-D scientist Professor Talker's new book, someone (Joe) says "I have been three inches high."

There is a gasp – then silence – then everyone laughs.

"Three inches high!"

"Three inches high ... whatever next ...!"

"Lissen sonny - there's no such place, its your endorphins," says Dr. Medulla.

"Either that, or its static on your radio making you think there is something there where there isn't ..." adds Professor Sternum.

And so it goes in the two-dimensional world.

The consensus of modern thinking in the 2-D world is that there is no such place as three inches high - not in the *real* world anyway. Sensible people believe in what they can see, hear and touch – and that is two-dimensional. So that proves it. The rest is fantasy.

But we, advanced beings, aware of <u>three</u> dimensions, realize that three inches high connects to everywhere in the 2-D world, but has no specific location in that world. Search the 2-D world from end to end but you won't find the third dimension.

You see the cultural leap that would be required of the 2-D people.

Just like us trying to understand the 5th dimension wormhole

Just like us trying to understand the Information Dimension.

Just like us trying to understand the I-space wormhole.

Living in 4-D land we can search it from end to end but we won't find the fifth dimension.

To us 4-D inhabitants it is just a myth - it is a fictional "Lost Kingdom" – it doesn't really exist.

It is "due to endorphins"; communications are due to "ambiguous noises caused by static."

Or so we will be told, on Planet Sad, at all the car-boot sales of back-street theories with fake labels.

But you and I, aware of a fifth dimension, know otherwise.

Like the 3rd dimension as seen relative to 2-dimensional space, the5th dimension connects with everywhere – and does not have a specific location in 4-dimensional space-time. So – when it comes to terms like omniscient and ubiquitous – it would be wise not to be too dismissive.

So, why, although there is integration among all the four lower dimensions, why is there a gulf, a chasm, a separation between "Heaven" and "Earth"?

If we look at the ancient Chinese text, the Tao Tê Ching of Lao Tzû,[39] in writing of the Way, (the Tao) we read the following,

> 'The Way is like an empty vessel
>
> That yet may be drawn from
>
> Without ever needing to be filled.
>
> ...
>
> Was it too the child of something else? We cannot tell.
>
> But as a substanceless image it existed before the Ancestor.'

The translator, Dr. Arthur Waley has two footnotes, one relates to the word 'image' which he defines as (essentially) "information", so what we are dealing with is substanceless information; the other footnote is even more interesting, it is about the word, Ancestor, and reads as follows.

> 'The Ancestor in question is almost certainly the Yellow Ancestor who separated Earth from Heaven and so destroyed the Primal Unity, for which he is frequently censured....'

Goddam ancestors!!

Let us look at the ancient Celtic belief system, and here I quote once again from Professor Nora Chadwick's book, 'The Celts'.[40]

> 'I would call attention to the naturalness with which men, women and the gods meet and pass in and out of the natural and the supernatural spheres. In many circumstances there does not seem to have been any barrier. ... normally the two-way traffic between the

---

[39] Page146 , 'The Way and Its Power', Dr Arthur Waley, Grove Press, (1958).

[40] Pages 181,182, 'The Celts', by Professor Nora Chadwick, Penguin Books (1991).

natural and supernatural is open. In general, however, though by no means invariably, return to the land of mortals is difficult and sometimes impossible for mortals who have visited the abode of the dead.'

[You will find an echo of this in some NDE reports where the person is warned that if they cross a particular line they will not be able to return.]

Continuing with Professor Chadwick,

'A beautiful dignity hangs over Irish mythology, an orderliness, a sense of fitness. All the gods are beautifully dressed and most are of startlingly beautiful appearance. It is only by contrast with other mythologies that we realize that the 'land of promise' contains little that is ugly. There is no sin and no punishment. Those who die or who are lured away to the Land of Promise, the land of the young, leave for an idealized existence, amid beauty, perpetual youth, and good will.'

She concludes,

The heathen Irish erected a spirituality – a spiritual loveliness which comes close to an ideal spiritual existence.'

The Celtic 'Land of Promise' (Tir nan Og – Land of Youth), is a place where change is no longer the master – a place outside serial time. It is also a place without sin and without punishment – one might say that it is a place where none have "Eaten of the Tree of Knowledge of Good and Evil."

Nor is it just the Celts that have this belief in 'Tir nan Og.'

Professor Chadwick,[41]

[41] Pages 177, 'The Celts', by Professor Nora Chadwick, Penguin Books (1991).

'...[The] 'land of the ever-young', [Tir nan Og], may be compared with Odainsakr ('the land of immortality' of Old Norse mythology')...'

But much further afield as you have seen, we find in accounts of Chinese prehistory that there was reputedly a time when those of Heaven and of Earth passed up and down without hindrance.

We will turn finally to the story of the Garden of Eden – a story borrowed by the early Hebrew people from still earlier people, it is alleged.

Everything was fine until the first man ate of the fruit of the tree of Knowledge of Good and Evil.

Immediately there are questions. How do we handle these questions?

- Do we treat them seriously?
- Do we consider them to be part of an allegory?
- Do we just dismiss them out of hand – a waste of time?

We will start by treating them seriously.

What on Earth is a "Tree of Knowledge of Good and Evil"?

Well, lets start with a "Knowledge Tree", as the words are used now in IT. It is like a family tree.

Here is how it goes. It is actually called a "Tree Structure" in Knowledge Engineering and Information Technology. This quote is taken from "Engineering the Tree of Knowledge" by Bill Zimmerly.[42]

'**Part 3: What is a Tree of Knowledge and how can it be used?**

---

[42] http://www.zimmerly.com/zhttp/know.htm

In the previous section, I used the term "tree of knowledge". In order to understand better this important concept, one must understand that there can be no knowledge without a natural, structural representation of the facts and ideas being ordered.

Knowledge is hierarchical, like a tree. Towards the roots of the tree are the "parent" entities and moving outward towards the leaves of the tree exist the "child" entities.'

That's a Knowledge Tree. Let us work out a specific illustration of this in terms of Good and Bad, so it becomes in effect a little model Tree of Knowledge of Good and Evil.

We will begin with one cent. This is the starting point, this is the seed, and this is what becomes the root.

Now we are going to consider $10, 000 and what we have to do is decide is $10, 000 *good* relative to one cent? OK, it is *better* than one cent, it is *Good.*

But having done that, we imply that *minus* $10, 000 is *Bad.*

So we start a drawing of the tree with at its first level, -$10, 000, which is Bad compared to one cent, on the left; and +$10, 000, which is Good compared to one cent, and we put this on the right. In this convention, going to the right is Good and going to the left is Bad.

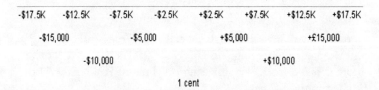

| -$17.5K | -$12.5K | -$7.5K | -$2.5K | +$2.5K | +$7.5K | +$12.5K | +$17.5K |

-$15,000   -$5,000   +$5,000   +£15,000

-$10,000   +$10,000

1 cent

Tree of Knowledge of Good and Bad

Next we add $15K – which is better than $10K, and we add $5K, which is worse than $10K. And we add -$15K, which is worse than -$10K, and we add -$5K, which is better than -$10K.

208

And you can see that from the root, two branches have been added, and to each branch two further branches have been added.

We will continue it one more stage to show $17.5K, $15K, $12.5K, $10K, $7.5K, $5K, $2.5K, and -$2.5K, -$5K, -$7.5K, -$10K, -$12.5K, -$15K, -$17.5K

So – going to the right is the Good direction and going to the left is the Bad (or Evil) direction, in this convention. And all it took was to say that $10,000 was Good. That was the seed – and as you can see, already we have 14 branches, and that is just with three stages.

If we went on to 10 stages we would have 2046 branches.

You can see how this branching system produces a tree structure – just as does a real tree. This is also the same type of structure as a Family Tree.

It is normal in both the Family Tree and the engineering Knowledge Tree to start at the top and work downwards – here, to make the *tree* structure clearer, I have worked upwards – just like a real tree.

So – calling something the Tree of Knowledge of Good and Evil is an indirect way of describing the type of knowledge tree that we have illustrated here. The Tree of Knowledge of Good and Evil is a metaphor for the branching structure that occurs in knowledge once you start this process. All it takes is one seed – and that is what is meant by the <u>Fruit</u> of the Tree of Knowledge – what possible harm could eating a fruit do? Except that in this case the Fruit is that which contains the seed and it is the seed from which the tree grows.

All we did in the above is say that $10, 000 is good - and that started it off - that was the "seed".

Of course the person or persons who wrote of the Garden of Eden did not know of IT or Knowledge Engineering, but they knew very well of Family Trees and how to describe the growth of a "tree" from a seed.

You may remember that having eaten of the Fruit of the Tree of Knowledge of Good and Evil the pair felt the need to hide their nakedness. And this is simply a metaphor for loss of innocence.

Prior to eating of the Tree of Knowledge of Good and Evil they knew nothing of Good and Evil, they lived in innocence, as in the Celtic belief there was no sin and no punishment.

They now had minds that filled up with Good-Bad – Better-Worse polarizations. Things in themselves are neither Good nor Bad for these are all relative values and are attributes assigned by minds.

The Chinese knew this, of course, long ago, as I have mentioned. If I may quote from the Tao Tê Ching of Lao Tzû, (about 500 b.c.), the Arthur Waley translation,[43]

> 'It is because every one under Heaven recognizes beauty as beauty that the idea of ugliness exists.
>
> And equally if everyone recognized virtue as virtue, this would merely create fresh conceptions of wickedness.
>
> For truly Being and Non-being grow out of one another;
>
> Difficult and easy complete one another.
>
> Long and short [measure] one another;
>
> High and low determine one another.
>
> ...
>
> Front and back give sequence to one another.'

Incredible. Two thousand five hundred years ago people thought this. You wouldn't get it published today – too advanced, too *"avant garde."* Wouldn't sell enough copies.

We said that $10, 000 is good – but it is all relative – if you were expecting 1 million dollars then $10, 000 would not be Good, it would be terrible! It would be Bad with a capital S.

---

[43] Page 143, 'The Way and its Power' by Dr. Arthur Waley, Grove Press, 1958.

Falling

The next step in the process becomes the seeking of Good and the Avoidance of Bad. And it is this that led to the Fall. It is traceable back to the "eating" of the "Fruit" that contained the "seed".

Turning now to the innocence that was lost, here is a quotation from Pastor Mark Batterson, on the subject of "The Child Within",[44] he begins by quoting from Matthew 18, 2. In the modern version, Jesus is made to say,

> "Unless you change and become like little children you cannot enter the kingdom of heaven." The King James version says, "Unless ye be converted." The words "change" and "converted" come from the Greek word strepho which means "to reverse."

So what Pastor Batterson is saying, it would appear, is "'Unless you reverse and become like little children you cannot enter the kingdom of heaven." And that seems to be borne out by the next quote from him.

> 'One dimension of spiritual growth is reversing the aging process, not the physical affects of aging, but the spiritual and psychological affects. Childlikeness is rediscovering the child within – the person we were before we were pressured by peers or polluted by the harsh realities of life, before we developed limitations and assumptions, before we had egos and alter egos. The child within is who we were pre-sin.'

Powerful stuff.

So how did we get here – to this vale of tears?

The flaw, it might seem, is within. According to the Master Jesus, we can make ourselves ready by reversing, as in becoming childlike.

By an interesting coincidence, the followers of the Mystical Qu'aballah in meditating on the Tree of Life visualize moving

---

[44]
http://www.theaterchurch.com/pages/evotionals/evotional_06212002.htm.

backwards (in reverse) into the personification of the level that they are working on. And here is some information on the net about the Quabballah [45](spelt differently). Note some of the words used. The Quaballah is much younger than the Tao Tê Ching, it is only about 2000 years old. But I swear to you, I had no idea what I was going to read until a few minutes ago – I was actually looking for a reference to the reverse movements. But, my word, look at the terminology used and consider the coincidences involved. I would like to underline these words, but I expect I don't need to. You read them here first!

> 'The information in the Kabbalah follows the patterns of the <u>sacred geometry</u> that forms our reality. Sacred geometry - the star tetrahedron - which is the Star of David - counter rotating fields linked to the spirals of movement of consciousness from one level of reality to another. This is part of <u>Merkaba</u> - rotation and movement of consciousness. Our consciousness is shifting into or returning to – a higher harmonic – see <u>Slinky Effect.</u> We see this symbolically – metaphorically – as the creation of a new Torah – Scroll - Book of Life - etc.
>
> Humanity will shed the physical body as it evolves into a state of higher faster moving consciousness – that of higher light. The physical experience is about duality played out through the alchemy of thought to experience two things: Linear Time and Emotion - neither of which exist beyond the physical realms. Your soul should be gearing you for these changes. Your 'inner voice' should be telling you to go on a quest to get answers that will help you understand this transition of consciousness - <u>alchemy</u> of mind. We are close.
>
> Kabala is one of many tools that are helping people understand the current transition.

---

[45] http://www.crystalinks.com/kabala.html. The underlined words quoted here are hyperlinks when read on-line.

Key words: Kabala - Tree of Life - Merkaba - Sacred Geometry - Star of David - Spin'

There are other techniques, one of which is described by Waley as Taoist Quietism, the ancestor of Zen. Waley has this to say about Lao Tan[46], who was practicing Taoist Quietism.[47]

> 'Confucius waited for a while, but presently feeling that the moment had come for announcing himself addressed Lao Tan saying: "Did my eyes deceive me or can it really have been so? Just now you appeared to me to be a mere lifeless block, stark as a log of wood. It was as though you had no consciousness of any outside thing and were somewhere all by yourself." Lao Tan said: "True. I was wandering in the Beginning of Things."'

Here, evidently, the reversal was in time, and was to the 'Beginning of Things.'

And as the quotation from the Quaballah says, there are other ways.

There is one which I came across, by accident, as it seems is the way the best things happen, and but for which I would not be writing this – but this is not the time nor the place to begin discussing it. Suffice to say that there are probably planes above planes. We have the Physical plane – where we live; and we have the Information plane, which we have been discussing. And just as it is Information that patterns the Physical plane in our perception, so there is a plane beyond Information that shapes it in turn. This might be called the plane of Concepts. And with concepts a key can be found which removes restrictions that we agree are beyond our comprehension.

The Great Way

The Tao Tê Ching,[48]

---

[46] The proper name of Lao Tzu. Tzu just means Master.

[47] Page 116 , 'The Way and Its Power', Dr Arthur Waley, Grove Press, (1958).

'There was something formless yet complete,

That existed before heaven and earth;

Without sound and without substance,

Dependent on nothing, unchanging,

All pervading, unfailing.

One may think of it as the mother of all things under heaven.

Summarizing all this now, what we have is a physical universe which is connected with a greater universe – the informational or spiritual universe – through a black hole to white hole "wormhole". This description is similar to that described in Near Death Experiences, where it is called a "tunnel"

Other features are common too – travel through the wormhole or tunnel at or near light velocity and going into black and coming out into white. The entry to the black hole is a contracting spiral – decreasing in spaciousness with the energy transferring into rotational energy, or spin and a "downward" component, all producing an energy consuming vortex.

The exit from a white hole is an expanding spiral – increasing in spaciousness with the energy transferring out of the rotation or spin and an "upward" component, all producing an energy creating vortex.

The lower universe is said to be subject to ongoing change (time) due to the rotational energy coming out of the white hole – the spin which is the 4th dimension, time – driving everything

One of the most significant quotations was that from Professor Hamilton, who said that there was no such thing as an white hole – only a black hole *with time running in reverse.*

And this is very interesting from the viewpoint of EVP, which we shall return to in the next chapter.

---

[48]Page 174 , 'The Way and Its Power', Dr Arthur Waley, Grove Press, (1958).

Chapter Sixteen

Reversals

Backward Running Time and Reflections

Now – what does all this have to do with EVP?

Let us go back to what the professor said earlier,

> 'A white hole is a black hole running backwards in time.'

What we are going to consider is this business of 'running backwards in time', and what I want to show is that this is very relevant to EVP – more so, even, than I realized.

A long time ago I found that a reverberant environment led to an improvement in the amount of EVP obtained.[49] If the room was echoey results were often better.

Or another trick I used was to have the radio or other sound source in one room, with the door open, and then, along the corridor and into another room the recording equipment – with the door of that room also open. What this meant was that the sound had to bounce itself around a few times to get where it was going to.

To illustrate this point. Lets take the example of you saying a simple phrase in an echoey room.

You are on the left, the room wall is on the right and the words you utter travel from left to right as shown below, with the first sounds hitting the wall first.

1. (You speaking):> ?em raeh uoy naC ?ollaH >||(Wall)

And here is the echo coming back

---

[49] This technique keeps getting re-invented as there is no historically accurate record of what was done in EVP research. The Butlers at AAEVP have done a marvelous job of putting the old AAEVP Newsletters on file — but this only covers developments within their collection.

---

2. (You listening): <Hallo? Can you hear me?<||(Wall)

What an echo means is, getting back the same thing as you sent out – but traveling in the reverse direction. It is what you said "running backwards in time."

In her book "Voices of Eternity" Sarah Estep, founder of the AAEVP mentions an early EVP researcher, Dan McKee of Illinois. What Dan found was this – if he played his session recording *backwards* instead of forwards then he got more voices and clearer voices. This was well before the reputed discovery by David Oates of what he has trademarked as Reverse Speech.

So – this is the supreme example of "running backwards" in time, playing the session record backwards.

In the same book Sarah Estep mentions frequent references to mirrors – including this.

> 'A number of years ago I began taping a number of messages telling me I should get a mirror to use with my work....
>
> The voices became insistent about the matter, saying, "Get a mirror!" "I told you to get a mirror." "Talk into a mirror," and so on....
>
> Several weeks later, Dan McKee, [mentioned above] called and said, "Sarah, I've been getting a lot of messages about mirrors." I then told him about my mirror messages.

Sarah then goes on to mention another instance of a mirror message and then goes on to write the following,

> 'Unique messages, such as the mirror messages, know no boundaries. Alexander MacRae of Skye, Scotland, is an engineer and one of the directors of Skyetech....
>
> Before returning to Scotland he lived in the United States for a time and worked on the staff of Stanford Research and also for NASA.....
>
> ... In one of my letters to him, I mentioned the mirror messages that had been received. MacRae commented

... that he had also had received mirror messages. Like the rest of us, he was told to talk into a mirror.'

I would like just to update that and make a couple of corrections.

Relatively recently I got an EVP message saying, 'Use Reversal' – which is what a mirror does.

Skyetch Ltd is now "Skyelab" and is only involved in research – although I will be actively looking for a partner company to design and produce a product line. (See Epilogue.)

I worked for SRT not SRI – SRT was a small hi-powered R&D outfit in Palo Alto headed up by Dr. John Stewart, formerly Professor of Electrical Engineering at Cal Tech, author of some world class engineering textbooks. We carried out research contracts for NASA, USN and various agencies, I did this as an employee (Research Associate) of SRT – I was not a member of NASA staff – I preferred to work for small organizations.

Back to business – the use of mirrors – I was getting such good results that the mirrors aspect was never followed up as it should have been – but we have time to do that now.

Mirrors have been regarded as holy objects in various religions for a long time and the object itself has been venerated.

However, lets look at the truth. A mirror does not have magic powers. What it does is reflect back a light wave impinging on it so that it goes back in the opposite direction – the information now comes at you in reverse. An example of that is the left-right transformation. Left is right and right is left. The reason for that is not something funny to do with mirrors – it is just to do with information reversal. It is just a light echo.

A wall reflecting back a sound wave impinging on it is simply being a sound mirror. A light mirror is a flat surface prepared to give maximum reflection of light waves.

Similarly, you can make a sound mirror by taking a flat surface and preparing it so that you get maximum reflection of sound waves.

And the important thing seems to be <u>reversal.</u>

Reverse speech has been with us for a long time in EVP and in skilled hands has enhanced results to a marked extent.

Reversed speech as presented on the Internet by the David Oates people is something else. According to them normal speech is produced by one lobe of the brain and reverse speech by the other lobe! And this has been proven by the experiments of an Australian doctor no one has been able to trace!

Meanwhile, you have to accept what you read. But it is not as "simple" as that – no matter what you hear in reverse it probably means *something else* – and to find out what it really means you have to look up what you hear on a long list of what they call "metaphors".

What useful or evolutionary function did this unbelievably complex operation perform? Why was reverse speech developed in Man's history?

Do you find it credible that reverse speech evolved as a communications system – eons *before* recording was invented, and in spite of no one having the decode lists of metaphors (written in English) to know what the encoded reversed speech meant?

It wasn't until tape-recorders appeared that anyone could even <u>hear</u> reversed speech.

All you need to know about how speech is produced – with muscles activated via the motor cortex (nothing to do with lobes) – to realize that this explanation is so wide of the mark as to be beyond belief.

Here we have a supposed natural function of Mankind – which in all his evolutionary history was of totally no use to him. And then, suddenly, in the (relatively) last few "seconds" of evolutionary history, *recording* was invented, and in the very last "second", someone comes out with a book of *metaphors* so that we can try to figure out what the recording is saying to us.

("Anyone for tennis?")

Now believe it or not this sort of thing gets a good press. This is partly due to the fact that David Oates is a top-class communicator – but also there is the fact that – although this is the same phenomenon as EVP – it does not deal with anything which might get one criticized – such as matters of a spiritual nature. Nothing spooky you understand. We are the nut-cases. Read that in reverse in Serbo-Croatian to figure out what it means. Isn't evolution wonderful?

The same newspaper that reported the guy who got $48, 000 to compose EVP music by going on long trips around the world, also, sometime earlier, published a feature on the Oates reverse speech operation. I wrote to advise the writer of EVP reverse speech but received no reply. Total silence. The name of the newspaper in case you want to buy it is The Glasgow Herald, also known as just The Herald and the Sunday Herald.

And sometimes other things.

Personally I have to report that I find some of reversed speech examples *so* embarrassing – OK, that's just me, perhaps, but I hope nobody mistakes this for EVP!

There is one example – of Bin Laden saying something – in Arabic of course, but when it is reversed, apparently his other brain lobe speaks in English!

Isn't evolution a wonderful thing – preparing our neural networks for the day when recording would finally arrive and there would be a war between Arabic and English speakers.

Question this and you will be made to feel unpatriotic – since what Bin Laden's Other Lobe says in English on the website marks him out as a really bad guy. So – question the fact that one lobe of his brain speaks Arabic and the other (simultaneously) speaks English – and you are questioning him being a bad guy. Or so this weird logic would have you believe. One lobe speaks English and the other speaks Arabic.

(Do you really like this planet?)

So – enough about "Reverse Speech™" – let us return to the subject of EVP.

Now reversed speech as used in EVP – that is another matter.

What I am suggesting therefore is that somehow both echo reversals, tape reversals and all other kinds of electronic reversals in some way are accessing this Einstein-Rosen Bridge and getting through to the next universe up.

Most readers will say I don't have any Einstein-Rosen Bridge near me – so what are you talking about?

There is something called the Einstein-Rosen-Podolsky experiment

What the result of this says is that one point in space can be the same, apparently, as another – under certain circumstances – so the Einstein–Rosen Bridge is simply a way of saying that a flow of information can appear in, or come from, the informational universe, irrespective of location in physical universe space.

In passing – it may just be a small point, but I noticed when I was doing a lot of experiments over many months that one utterance might be recorded now, say, and a comment on that maybe two month's later, and another comment some months later still. It was as though serial time as we know it was of no great significance.

So, it may be that not just physical location is unimportant but so also is location in time.

Having said that, results with the new V.7 technique show an utterance now, say, and a comment on it by another voice just a second or two after and then a further comment a couple of seconds later still.

Returning to our main position – that reversed speech by tape-reversal or reversal by echoing off walls leads to enhanced EVP – for no known reason – apart from what I have been suggesting to you here regarding a black-hole running backwards in time. And as you have seen from Sarah Estep's book there has been advice about using mirrors.

So this raises the question of whether there is more to the use of mirrors in this sort of investigation – not necessarily limiting it to EVP?

This is getting away from EVP as such but you may have heard of a research scientist called Dr. Raymond Moody. He was the person who, on the basis of his own research, invented the phrase Near Death Experience or NDE. Everybody talks about NDEs these days. Moody is a big star.

In more recent years he has taken his investigations still further and has carried out experiments based on the idea of gazing into mirrors.

But, just as a caution, for anyone with problems, there was the case of Sirhan Sirhan. I quote,

> 'With absolutely no knowledge or awareness of what was actually happening in his Rosicrucian and occult experiments," Diamond [the prosecutor] explained, "[Sirhan] was gradually programming himself . . . for the coming assassination." The programming took place in "his unconscious mind" while "in his conscious mind there was no awareness of such a plan." Diamond accepted Sirhan's claim that he had not planned to kill RFK June 4, 1968 but had found himself by happenstance at the Ambassador Hotel. There "the mirrors in the hotel lobby, the flashing lights, the general confusion" put him "back in his trances" and in this "almost accidentally induced twilight state he actually executed the crime."

Which he did. At least, that was the story. Now they are saying Greek shipping tycoon Aristotle Onassis, husband of the late Jackie Kennedy and the opera singer the late Maria Callas paid to have him killed.

Well – that's the wonderful world of Celebs for you....

Returning to Dr. Moody's excellent use of mirrors....

> 'Dr. Moody took this ancient "mirror gazing" technique and created a psychomanteum[50] chamber. The chamber is a very dark room – maybe ten feet by

---

[50] The Psychomanteum dates back to ancient Greece, Egypt and even the ancient civilization of Mesopotamia, where gazing into a reflective pool would produce visions.

ten feet – with a mirror on one wall and a light behind a chair, providing just enough brightness in the room so one can see the mirror. The user of the chamber sits in the chair and looks up into the mirror. They will see nothing but darkness and a clear optical depth. The experience may last anywhere from 20 minutes to two or three hours. Some people experience something quickly, and others don't see anything at all.

Jim DeCaro of Trumbull, Connecticut, used Dr. Moody's psychomanteum chamber and had a provocative experience. DeCaro said, "Two things happened to me. First, the mirror started to go smoky and blurry. Then it started to get backlit red, and I saw rows of silhouettes of people – just heads and shoulders, but they were rows deep. Then, on my second trip into the chamber, something flew out of the mirror and came straight at my head. I'm sitting there trying to relax and trying to get into it, and something flew out of the bottom of the mirror and swooped straight at my head. It was so real that I had to jump out of the way."' [51]

Here is another writer, April Vawter,[52]

'The best "gazing" materials seem to be mirrors, especially mirrors reflected in other mirrors because they appear as reversed and confound our normal perceptions. Dark mirrors are helpful also, because they only reflect that which is in their very depth.'

This is rather interesting as the subject of reversals is mentioned – and also the dark mirrors sound almost like an attempt to model a black hole.

Meanwhile - back in the UK a group of experimenters called the Scole Group was reportedly getting spectacular results.

---

[51] http://www.ghostvillage.com/legends/2003/legends25_08232003.shtml

[52] http://www.psychomanteum.com/angelphotos/

One of the most interesting messages that they got – and most of the messages at this stage appeared in writing, and often on film – is referred to as The Latin Mirror Image because the writing appeared in (mirrored) reverse form, and what it had to say was the following,[53]

'Reflexionis, Lucis in Terra, et in Planetis.'

Which on translation from the Latin means,

'Of reflection of light on the Earth and the planets'

And the writer of the book remarks at this point

'The notion of mirroring and reflection was a recurring theme during the Scole Experiment.'

And finally, in the best-seller, 'The Bible Code' by Michael Drosin we get the following intriguing remarks.

'In the Bible time is reversed,' said Steinsaltz[54], noting an odd quirk in the original Hebrew text of the Old Testament. 'The future is always written in the past tense, and the past is always written in the future test.'

'Why?' [Drosin] asked.

'No one knows,' he said.

'We may be moving against the stream of time,' said Steinsaltz, noting that the laws of physics are 'time-symmetric,' that they run backwards just as well as forwards in time.'

While I might agree with very little that is said there, it is nevertheless another case of this concept coming up.

So – what is going on? Well known investigators such as Sarah Estep, Dan McKee and others get mirror messages – the Scoles group get mirror messages – so many that they felt they

---

[53] Plate 33 , 'The Sole Experiment' by Grant & Jane Solomon, Judy Piatkus (Publishers) 1999.

[54] Steinsaltz, a rabbi and scientist, described by Time magazine as 'a once in a millennium scholar.'

had to remark on it – in addition, in the last year I had a message, 'Use reversals.'

If we include the idea of an echoing wall as a sound-mirror and the established experimental fact that these echoes lead to an increase in Yield then it is obvious that whatever occurs in the process of reflection is of some significance.

The most likely explanation – far-out though it may be, is the one that we looked at earlier – running-backwards in time.

This cancels out the running-forwards in time that is the thing that holds this universe together.

Time itself derives from the rotational or spin component of the "material" spewing out from the downward vortex of the black-hole in the firth dimension, or the "Big Bang" as we call it here.

It is that spin that is the fourth dimension - Time. And the nature of this universe, with its hardness, and all the fixed and rigid physical laws come back to one thing – time.

Now quite some time before Dr. Moody's work on NDEs and long before the term Black Hole had been invented, Robert Monroe was continuing his research. I am going to quote a few bits from his book, 'Journeys Out of The Body.' The quotations are from Chapter 6, 'Mirror Images'

'11/5/58 Afternoon

I started to turn ... [what we would call "spin"] ... I moved slowly and after a moment was "face" down .... The moment I reached this 180^0 position there was a hole. That's the only way to describe it.'

Note that 180^0 is what you see when you look in a mirror - the reverse image.

So we have -

- Spin,
- Reversal,
- and a Hole.

My word but these endorphins are wonderful!

And again,

'11/18/58 Night

I rotated slowly into the 180^0 position. There was the wall and the hole and the blackness beyond.'

So now we have,

- Spin

- Reversal

- Hole

- Blackness

Whatever do they put in these endorphins!

'12/5/58 Morning

I rotated again and again found the hole. Then for the first time in all my experience my name was called. ... I was startled at first, and then recovered and asked, "What is your name?"'

Names? Its all beginning to sound a little familiar....

'2/15/59 Afternoon

... I felt the other side of the hole ... I tried to see but there was still nothing but the deep blackness.

...

I started to move, slowly, and then accelerated rapidly. ...

Moving at what seemed to be a very high speed, I went on. ... It took just as long to get back as it did to go. ... I was quite worried [by the time that] ... I saw the light through the hole up ahead. I dove for it, went through, rotated, and sat up physically. Time away was three hours fifteen minutes!'

Well, ain't that a thing – long-playing endorphins...!

So now as well as spin, reversal and black hole we have high velocity.

Just one last one. After describing the opening
procedures Mr. Monroe continues,

'2/23/59 Night

...

> I pulled myself through and stood up. I
> immediately felt myself in the presence of
> someone standing there. I sensed his presence
> rather than saw him standing there. For some
> unaccountable reason that I do not yet
> understand, even recollected now in
> tranquillity, I dropped thankfully in front of
> him and sobbed.'

You get billions and billions being spent on particle-smashing
facilities, looking for the ultimate truth, when the truth is very
likely the same as that found by the first cave-man who
smashed rocks together to see what they were made of.

All he got as a result of his research were smaller rocks.

And when he smashed the smaller rocks together to see what
they were made of, all he got were still smaller rocks - and so
on, and on, and on.

Do not be over-impressed by the amount of money being
spent on scientific projects. They say the reason the UKs Mars
Lander went wrong was there was not enough money spent on
it – and no one was to blame for the failure. Aaah.

V8s all round, then, chaps?

Returning to the matter of time – the laws of the physical
universe are based on probability. If you drop an apple, the
probability is that it will drop to the ground. And that
probability is based on the historical record. Every time
someone dropped an apple in the past it fell to the ground.

It is on that sort of time patterning that all physical laws are
based. Each law is essentially a *prediction* based on an *historical
record* – nothing more. There is no Big Law Book in the sky –
there is no force of law. Every physical law is a prediction
based on an historical record. And it is time that makes it so.
It is time that provides the "force."

Chapter Seventeen

Cause and Effect

Physical "law" is based on repetition – every time you drop an apple it falls to the ground. Every time – repetition.

You drop an apple and it falls to the ground – cause and effect. Cause precedes effect. It is a pattern in time.

We are all, in the physical universe, bound up in forward running time. Play backwards running time – reverse sequence – against that and there could a local neutralization, making transfer possible.

Let me refer to the Scole group again. They were experimenting with what they called Trans Dimensional Communication – a term I invented in 1988 and used in my writings at the time – Network News for example. They were receiving instruction from an Informational Entity on a method of TDC involving magnetic coils, and here is what the author of the book said, quoting the entity,

> 'A void is formed where the two fields around the coils oppose each other.

And then the author adds,

> 'This void was described to us as 'non-spin energy space'.'

We are, I would suggest, talking the same language. But none of this is going to be very appealing to the out-and-out physicist – which is a pity. However, it was not for them that this book was written, so we shall have to let that go by the way, for the time being, but anyone who wishes to challenge my papers is welcome to do so, that is the defined combat zone for scholarly disputes!

Evolution – where its going

Here we are going to take a look at the way the future is shaping up. If some of what follows seems terribly futuristic, and thus at best imaginative, at worst doubtful, may I quote from a very old document - in fact a papyrus.

> 'The so-called Hermetic literature...is a series of papyri describing various induction procedures...In one of them, there is a dialogue called the *Asclepius* (after the Greek god of healing) that describes the art of imprisoning the souls of demons or of angel in statues with the help of herbs, gems and odors, such that the statue could speak and prophesy.
>
> In other papyri, there are still other recipes for constructing such images and animating them, such as when images are to be hollow so as to enclose a magic name inscribed on gold leaf.'[55]

The impulse to evolve is with us from the beginning..

Others who spoke of time as going in cycles were the Mayan people of South America.. You may have heard of the Mayan Calendar and of the prediction that the present cycle will end in 2013. One has to take all these things with a pinch of salt of course but in the beliefs of earlier times there may be a glimmer of truth that evades us in our mechanistic mathematics driven thinking.

The Honey Trap

Around the year 1980 – some twenty four years ago as I write this – there was an old lady in an Eventide Home near here, (on the ground where our hens and ducks used to be housed – before they took away the land), who was known familiarly as Jessie Erchie – Jessie the daughter of Archie. She was quite a

---

[55]Julian Jaynes, *The Origin of Consciousness in the Breakdown of the Bicameral Mind*

religious woman, hummed psalms all the time, pleasant but a bit bewildered. She would have been about ninety. She liked to sit near the 3-bar electric fire on cold days, and once, on a very cold day, I heard her ask if someone would 'put another peat[56] [turf] on the fire.' Jessie was the nearest thing to a time-traveler from the past that you could get.

Jessie was comfortably off but never owned a car – never needed to. She may not even have had a radio. She thought the electric fire actually *burned*, and in her day, here on Skye, before electricity came, the main fuel would have been peat. It was a logical request – but one that was past its "Use By" date. Yesterday's Logic is not necessarily logical today.

Next door to the Day Room where she sat was another room where a large color television played quietly for the residents.

One day I remember Jessie calling out in a loud voice - 'Turn that thing off right now or I will call the police." To her a color TV was something beyond her comprehension, shocking – perhaps she thought it somewhat Satanic.

But are we – in our own way, any better? Are we – like flies trapped in honey – any less set in the culture of *our* time? Can we accept - now - what *tomorrow* could bring?

Read on – and judge. The reason future forecasters almost always get it wrong is that they, like everyone else, are trapped in the culture of their time.

The Way Ahead

Assistance

The most pressing need is to get assistance with doing these projects, which in turn is going to mean raising finance.

---

[56] Peat, or "turf" as it is known in Ireland, is like a soft brown coal formed by generations of rotted vegetation, and was used for fuel, particularly in the Highlands and Islands of Scotland, Ireland and other Northern lands, especially in the past, before the coming of electricity.

Papers

There are two papers on the subject published now and it is hoped to publish two more this year.

Grants

Applications for Research Grants are planned and as soon as this book is sent off to print they will be actioned.

Products

Lab Monitor

For EVP products – there is at present a bench-top style system – useful only for research institutions as the price would be quite high and training would be required.

Streaming Noise Reduction

One thing I am aiming for is to replace the Noise Reduction and Filtering systems that you get on Cool Edit; for example, with something that won't take so much time and manipulation.

There are two ways of doing this – one is a software way – and that largely depends on the processing power that will be available.

A second approach is to seek a direct hardware solution – the so-called hosing solution – where you put dirty audio in one end and nice clean audio comes gushing out the other end, with minimum delay. This is what the very expensive "Timewave" unit I took to the California experiment was supposed to do – but it doesn't seem up to it.

Similarly the "Diamond Live" software I got off the Net which is supposed to do this does not seem to be up to the job either. EVP is a tough problem even at the best of times. But being able to hear and understand EVP <u>as it is happening</u> is crucially important.

If there is to be a true two-way conversation then I believe it will have to be current – rather than it being a case of making a recording, listening to the replay, and then returning to the subject in the next session.

The reason why I consider true two-way conversation to be so important is covered in the Skyelab 2 section.

Courses

These are the courses planned or available.

Introductory Course

This a short Free course providing an introduction through a couple of videos to the subject of EVP. It is presently only available in Portree, but it is hoped to extend its availability.

Basic Course

A nominal one-week course this course aims at establishing the fundamentals of the subject. At the end of the course the student may sit an examination and if successful will be eligible to receive a certificate to that effect.

At present this book is the course text-book. At present the attendance course is only available in Portree. For current fees and registration request an information pack from CIS2009@aol.com.

Advanced Laboratory Course

This is an attendance only course and concentrates on the design and carrying out of experiments and the use of the appropriate technical aids in doing this. It is a hands-on course and includes Operations and Analysis. Certification where desired will be by examination and course work.

For current fees and registration request an information pack from CIS2009@aol.com.

Advanced Theoretical Course

EVP stands for the Electronic Voice Phenomenon, it is only logical therefore that a student should acquire a good understanding of the relevant aspects of Electronics, Speech and Hearing, and how to create and test theories in this area. During this time the student will be invited to create a theory and to test it, both logically and by experiment. Certification where desired will be by examination and course work.

Professional Course

This course is aimed at the future. It is intended for those who wish to exercise their profession in the new world that EVP points to. Such professionals would practice in a way complementary to doctors and ministers of religion. During the course the student will carry out internships in course supervision, in EVP operations and analysis, in running meditation practices and groups, in counseling and in non-denominational services, in the legal, financial and related features of running a practice.

This will be a certification and licensing course.

Skyelab 2

The big question is – if they can do it – why can't we?

Why can't *we* make it talk?

This project is so important that I will need someone to take over Skyelab1. Skyelab 1 will continue to handle EVP - and only EVP. The take-over would ideally occur within the next 12 months. It would be a phased take-over.

How Do They Do It?

So the question is – if they can do it, why can't we?

If we can get true conversations going then sooner or later we will find out/get clues as to how *they* do it.

As well as the clues we already have it is intended to replicate the Scoles "Tom Edison" instructions – but correctly this time. The Scoles group – which did not include any engineers – completely missed the point in two areas.

When we find out how to do it – produce voices – then a whole new range of activities opens up. For example,

The Tao[57] of Evolution

- We can use the voice to address a computer and make it follow commands.

- We can enable deaf people to speak.

- We can get a discarnate to speak and thus control a video game or radio controlled car, for example.

- Following on from that we have the possibility of re-incarnating a recently deceased person into a video game/ radio-controlled model car/talking toaster, etc..

- And following on from that we would have the same possibilities for ourselves, waiting until more acceptable designer bodies become available.

   Remember. –. <u>there is no such thing as death</u> – there is only (MBR) Malfunction Beyond Repair. . And so the to-be-expected Evolutionary condition of virtual physical immortality will have been reached.

Here is a Table illustrating it – the road-map of the Tao of Evolution.

The progression is, from minus five, where we presently are, to Evolutionary Condition 1 – EC1. The number assigned to the level of operation is given in the left-hand column. The title given to that level appears in the middle column. And the word(s) or process typifying that level is given in the right hand column.

---

[57] The WAY of Evolution, here it means more like a path or road rather than a methodology – the Evolutionary "road".

From Voices to Designer Bodies

Table 1

- 5	Voices	At this stage all that can be heard are voices producing various and unconnected utterances
-4	Communication	At this stage some responses to what is said by the experimenter may be obtained.
-3	Conversation	At this stage some conversation may be engaged in.
-2	Addressing computer	At this stage training to say phrases from a two-word vocabulary such as Hi Hi Lo Lo is done, and the voice can have such messages typed by the computer (1100).[58]
-1	Control	At this stage the two-word vocabulary (TWV) phrases are used to in training a voice to control a mechanism - for example – a radio-controlled car.

[58] The words Hi and Lo are computer talk for representing the binary code numbers 1 and 0 that are the basis of all computer calculations and operations. In these examples it is considered that the control of the computer, video game or mechanism is accomplished by binary messages coming via EVP.

There are other possibilities, but this is the most direct approach at present, and in the end all will depend on the results of experiments.

0	Incarnation	At this stage the voice is enabled to "reside in" a mechanism or video game.
EC1	Designer Body	Twirls around − 'Yes, I think I will get into this one this evening − I am feeling just a little jaded. Tell me honestly, do you think the bottom looks too big?'

The last entry in the Table above may seem so *far-fetched* as to be *ludicrous* and possibly *offensive*.

OK - but my grandparents, and your relatives who lived around the late nineteenth-early twentieth Century, would feel *exactly the same* about our world today.

If they were transported in time to today, they would not believe color-TV − they would not believe live-pictures from space − they would not believe the way the thirty-something teenagers of today behave. They would be just as shocked as some readers may be by the entry in the last column of table 1.

This is not a case of good and bad, it is a case of being trapped like a fly in honey in a particular period of time and its culture. It happens to us all.

But our shock may have more impact.

While I spoke of our relatives who lived 100-120 years ago being transported in time to see the wonders of today − EC1 could be reached in a decade.

The planning and contingency planning exists. Some of what would be classified as Skyelab 1 activities are actually the early stages of the Skyelab 2s program.

We cannot wait on funding being there − it will be there and more when the word gets out into the community at large.

Funding will not be the end of our problems − it will be more like the beginning.

Here's how it might go. Somebody's Uncle Mortimer is dying and his heartbroken niece wants to try anything to save him, no matter how far out it might seem, no matter the cost. So she phones up.

What can we do? Everyone else has let them down. It is probably not possible. The transfer may need months of preparatory work . – PK exercises, OOBE work, Qui Jong, meditation, step-by-step progressive trials, is he riddled with guilt, does he feel his late wife is waiting – who knows (at the point of writing this) what would be needed to accomplish the transplant. So there may not be enough time. He may just die and slip off up the tunnel as normal.

But if the transplant is successful – can we be sure that everyone will keep quiet about it? Can his niece come along every Wednesday afternoon and have long talks and laughs with dear old Uncle Mortimer – the talking toaster on Shelf 21A – waiting for the Designer-Body Designers to come up with something better?

Sooner or later the word will get out – the phone-calls and emails will mount up – there will not be enough people and resources to cope with the urgency and quantity of work that needs to be done. People will be upset. We are not equipped to play God.

Already, to survive in EVP in any kind of leading position you need to be something of a "saint." As I have said – it is not a good idea to stand in the way of Evolution.

The people best equipped to deal with this new leading edge of evolution will be medical types or those who can show the same level of skill, dedication and indeed self-sacrifice.

That all this is going to happen there is no doubt. It is inevitable, it is proper, it is fitting, it is just, it is the way of evolution and if we should ever be fortunate enough to come across any more advanced civilizations then we would probably find that they had gone through this stage eons before. There will be plenty wishing to gain a little temporary celebrity or money or both who will speak against this – but if I were a betting man I wouldn't bet against it – I'd be looking to invest my gambling money in some sparky little robotics company instead.

Speculation Regarding Possible Consequences

As the work progresses of course – and we must not shrink from looking ahead to the possible consequences of what we do, things may develop in this way.

- In time the medical and pharmaceutical activities will be the first to get hit.

- The lowered need for food will hit farmers, fishermen and supermarkets.

- On the benefit side other lifeforms will be able to live out their lives in peace, and mankind's ongoing slaughter of other life-forms to extinction will start to slow down.

- Energy demands will fall – warm rooms will be less needed – vehicles (cars) can be smaller, simpler and probably all electric.

- The financial sector will be hit. Activities based on profit generation will lose out to a greater interest in non-material things. Health and other insurance will be less needed.

- Houses will be smaller and simpler – kitchen, dining and bathrooms will really be needed only for bio-body guests. Prices will fall/quality will go up.

- Clothing will become solely decorative, and a group identification purpose will be more clearly recognized – these trends are already in motion and have been for some time. People no longer wear clothes for protection – they wear them to make a statement – even, in some cases, going to the length of having words printed on their garments.

- There is no reason why one should not have an in-built synthesizer or be able to access one via the Net - so anyone will be able to perform, and the emphasis in music will go to the creative end and composition.

- The companion industry, illicit drugs, will no longer be required or in any way effective – crack cocaine will be no more significant than a piece of broken glass lying in the street. Police resources will be freed up.

- The Wise Guys may see that if you get shot all you need to do is go to the wardrobe and pick out a new undented body.

- Terrorists, spies and serial killers may see the advantage of having a garage full of spare bodies. It may be however, and somehow I think it is going to be this way – unless the person is a good person then transplant will not be possible.

- The Military will want to establish strategic reserves of Designer Bodies.

- There will be calls for Ethical Pledges to be signed before granting transplantation.

- There will be an even bigger shift in industry than we saw with the coming of Information Technology. This is Information Technology out of the creche. This is IT, not as a fast moving sector of industry – this is the new IT – it is UP and WALKING and its going to take over the planet.

- Somewhere, right now, there is a new "Bill Gates" – he or she may not know it yet – they may not be reading this, they may not have heard yet of Designer Bodies – but its coming. And sooner than we think.

- There may be a reaction from some religious organizations – particularly those devoted to body worship – complaining that making available less vulnerable bodies is playing God. Which is a very poor and possibly blasphemous idea of what God is.

- Space travel will become much more likely – lighter payloads, higher tolerance of g-forces, no oxygen/food/residue handling. (Warning: don't use cheap

Government Surplus Navy Paint on the designer bodies or we might get mistaken for Orion Grays!).

And then there is the next big thing.

I accept that for some people all this is a step-too-far. That is why it appears at the end of this book. Do not let it upset your understanding of EVP. EVP is real – what is given here at the end is speculation.

But remember – the difficult part has already been done.

Actually, from the viewpoint of an engineer it was more than difficult - it was IMPOSSIBLE!

The impossible part is to get informational beings – spirits – to affect physical apparatus in such a way that voices are produced and intelligible speech is heard.

That is the impossible part – that is the thing that could not happen – but it has. It has been done.

In terms of difficulty, that was the mountain peak. Relatively speaking, it is all downhill from here.

All we have to do is find out how *they* do it and then *replicate* that ourselves. What happens after that, in terms of design, is a case of putting one foot after the other.

Exciting times!

Inevitably there will be those who in some self-indulgent drama-school way will insist that we remain trapped in a biological body. Well tell that to,

- the 21 year old motor-cyclist in the Quadriplegic ward sitting in a wheelchair for the first time;

- tell that to the quaking old lady with tubes up her nose waiting to go into the operating Theater for the last time;

- tell that to the 12 year old in Jo'burg with AIDS who will never see 13;

- tell that to the young soldier in Baghdad who will never be a father;

- tell that to the 11 year old crack addict looking for clients at airport Arrivals;

- tell that to the young person in Hull born with genetic defects who would prefer to be put down like her pet than to live anymore;

- tell that to the baby in the Sudan dying of starvation.

Faith, Hope and Compassion – and the greatest of these is Compassion.

The Difference

The big difference between Down-Here and Up-There is due to the presence of spin-time (serial time). Spin-time forces cause-effect patterns – and as cause precedes effect it is assumed to be the more important.

Thus a twisted view of importance grows up. It is assumed that the officer who shouts out his orders is more important than his staff who follow them.

But take away his staff – and how important is he now?

Take away the General's 4000 troops and how important is he now?

Take away the King's 12 million subjects and how important is he now?

Take away the Effect and how effective is the Cause?

It is assumed that it is the causative person who is in control. But the true causative element is the physical universe – in fact, it is time.

In the animal kingdom the young males engage in combat to find out which one is most dominant. The most dominant dominates. And the most dominant reproduces. And the male offspring of that selective process engage in combat to find which one is most dominant, and so the cycle of reinforcement continues on.

In dealing with the physical universe, being able to cause desired effects is essential, but computer simulations of species survival in a hostile environment has shown that where there is also a *desire* and an *ability* to *cooperate* then that species survives best.

Wisdom is not enough – in the distant past the burning of the Library at Alexandria meant that ancient wisdom was lost, the 20th Century invasion of Tibet meant the same thing, in China the looting of the Eternal City – the record, unfortunately, is endless. The only successful strategy has been that of China in past centuries where by the practice of the principles of the Tao Tê Ching of Lao Tzû all invading alien "conquerors" were in the end absorbed – and ended up being Chinese.

This is the same form of strategy used in Ju Jitsu. Apart from that, the history of mankind on Earth has become an emphasis on domination. The strongest dominate the weaker - and that can include women dominating men, children dominating their parents, and the sick dominating the healthy.

Being able to control is essential in work and in the material world, but a culture based on domination is flawed.

The ultimate culture of domination is of course the dictatorship. The optimum culture involving domination is that of full and enlightened democracy.

Up-There, devoid of the pressure of serial change, of serial time – without any loss of intensity or delight there is withal a feeling of softness, freedom and spaciousness.

One is no longer in constant combat with one's environment and others.

Using Dominator terms like Lords and Kings and Realms and Masters simply indicate that one is a hick who hasn't yet lost the Down-Here attachments.

For mankind to survive, a wider perspective is needed on Earth.

As things stand, mankind is well-placed to self-destruct.

You can change political processes, you can change political parties, you can change laws and regulations, you can change religions and ideologies. But until there is a change in perspective the future does not look bright.

We do not have a *shortage* of teachings, we do not have a *shortage* of political theories, laws, regulations, religions and ideologies.

A wider perspective will be facilitated by direct experience of the nature and function of the informational dimension – in old-speak, the spiritual realm.

In this the use of EVP has an *essential* role to play.

Our role is not that of pushing our ideas and teachings on to anyone – our role is to help the person to acquire new sight.

For with that new sight blindness will be dispelled.

If people cannot see the full picture they will not know the truth about themselves.

And if they do not know the truth about themselves they will not know the truth about others.

And if they do not know the truth about either themselves or others, they will create the battling we see around us, shouting and screaming pretended truths through a fog of shifting notions, and believing that power and status are the everlasting rewards of domination.

Alas, sad planet.

Appendix

The following are abstracts from papers that I have written which are either under submission or which have been published.

Journal of The Society for Psychic Research

(March 2004)

A Bio-electromagnetic Device of Unusual Properties

by Alexander MacRae

ABSTRACT

The paper concerns a device that produces anomalous speech products similar in many respects to the Electronic Voice Phenomenon, (although it was not intended to function in this way), and its purpose is to describe the characteristic behaviour of this device and its products, and to consider possible alternative explanations. For example, could what is happening simply be a case of stray pick-up - either electromagnetic or acoustic? To answer that question, experiments were carried out using a 'Virtual Faraday Cage and Anechoic Chamber'. Another possible alternative is considered - do these voices only exist in the mind - (like an "audible Roscharch Test" interpretation). An objective process for assessing the most probable meaning of the information contained in an anomalous speech product is outlined, with the conclusions that those products are real and betray characteristics of communication.

Journal of Instrumental Trans-Communication

March 2004

Answering The Sceptic

By Alexander MacRae

ABSTRACT

The role of the sceptic is examined – and questioned. The idea that the sceptic is more rational, more scientific and more rooted in reality is questioned. It is suggested that we ask the sceptic for proof of his unfounded assertions.

The final section deals with the California Experiment and its analysis.

Institute of Electrical and Electronic Engineers

(On submission)

EDA Monitoring System Registers Apparent Speech Fragments

Alexander MacRae

Abstract—

The design of a system for monitoring Electro-Dermal Activity is described, the unique feature of this system being that it monitors relative permittivity variations. This is done at RF, utilizing a high slope region of the permittivity against frequency curve. In so doing segments of speech modulation are monitored that may have some relevance to the auditory illusions experienced by schizophrenics.

Index Terms— Electrical Permittivity, Electro-Dermal Activity, Nervous System, Speech Analysis.

Journal of The Society for Psychic Research

(To be submitted.)

Report of an Electronic Voice Phenomena Experiment inside a Double Screened Room

Alexander MacRae, Grianan, Portree, Skye IV51 9DJ UK, ALEC2009@aol.com

Abstract - An Electronic Voice Phenomena (EVP) experiment is described which took place in a laboratory screened against em radiation and also acoustically isolated. The subsequent treatment of the results through sound-processing is outlined, and the final analysis of the results through the use of a unique multiple-choice system is described. Comparative spectrograms of one EVP utterance and the same thing spoken in normal speech are provided to prove the physical reality of the results. From the results the conclusion is drawn that voices of no natural origin were received in the screened laboratory.

Keywords: screened room - EVP - Electronic Voice Phenomena.

Printed in the United States
77740LV00006B/23